Praise for *A Revelation of Lo*

"How does the book of Revelatio... apply to your life today? Where are we on God's time table for the end of days?" John, the Revelator, gives us keys to God's end-time plan, but Jill Grossman gives us keys to understanding the revelation itself. And what's so beautiful is the mention of the word "love" more than 100 times in this gripping study, a reminder that Revelation is a love letter to us all, God's final one that will see us home. It is with a whole heart that I recommend to you the ministry, the life and the writings of Jill Grossman.

Laura Harris Smith
#1 Best-selling Author of
Seeing the Voice of God: What God is Telling You Through Dreams and Visions
Founding co-pastor of
Eastgate Creative Christian Fellowship, Nashville, Tennessee

The study guide is far more than a study guide… it's a very practical compassionate and informative "friend" that comes alongside any believer or Bible student needing a working relationship with the book of Revelation for these times. I cannot imagine how much time and thoughtfulness Jill Grossman put into its composition. It is a truly outstanding labor of love. It will surely unlock Revelation to people who never before were able to read it for it's contemporary and practical significance.

Randy Berg
Pastor of
Grace Church, LaVergne, Tennessee

I have had the pleasure and privilege of working with some truly gifted writers and teachers over the years, but I have to say that Jill Grossman is one of my favorites. Her deep insight, coupled with her straight-forward, easy to grasp exposition of the scriptures, makes this work both enlightening and engaging. If you are one of those who have longed to understand Revelation, but have been too intimidated to delve beyond the first few scriptures, this study companion is an absolute must for you.

Barbie Loflin
Assistant Pastor of
Springhouse Worship & Arts Center, Smyrna, Tennessee
Author of
Morning Mist
Positioned for Transition

A Revelation of Love is a window through the heart of a grace-full woman into one of the most formidable books in the New Testament, The Revelation of St. John. Jill Grossman has taken what, to many of us, is a quagmire of mystical metaphor and apocalyptic allegory, and made it a love letter as tender and as heartwarming as a note from a high school sweetheart. It is easy to read, and when laid beside the scripture portrays the real affection of the Father through the gift of His Son in every chapter. She takes personal stories, everyday experiences and a keen eye for meaning and makes Revelation a genuine love letter.

Jill is an amazingly gifted musician and actress, both professions that require the ability to interpret and communicate. She has brought those abilities to bear in this Biblical companion. You will have a new appreciation for the power and personality of the last book of the Bible. And you will be amazed once again at how God speaks His divine delight for us in every chapter. Open your Bible, take up this workbook and prepare to be loved all over again.

Dr. Mike Courtney
Founder and Director of
Branches Counseling Center
Author of
Failure and How I Achieved It
Laugh Lines
Person, Purpose and Power

Many books are available to the general reader claiming to provide insight into the book of Revelation. A lot of these books are filled with wild speculation and minimal research. Jill Grossman avoids the trap of claiming to unravel all the mysteries of the Apocalypse and instead focuses on the revelation of Christ and God's love. This book is highly recommended for those who desire solid background information for understanding Revelation while avoiding the speculative fancies of personal interpretive bias.

Ronnie Meek
Senior Pastor, Springhouse Worship & Arts Center, Smyrna, Tennessee

It is scholarly enough to keep the attention of the serious student and simple enough not be lost in the quagmire of end-times theology. *A Revelation of Love* is a breath of fresh air. It draws you into this *mystery* revealed and offers a rare glimpse into a book that most people avoid.

Rodney Boyd
Author of
Pro-Verb Ponderings

A REVELATION of Love

A REVELATION of Love

A COMPREHENSIVE STUDY COMPANION TO
THE BOOK OF REVELATION

BY

JILL GROSSMAN

WordCrafts

A Revelation of Love
  A Comprehensive Study Companion to the Book of Revelation
Copyright © 2015
Jill Grossman

Cover design and author photo by David Warren

Published by WordCrafts Press
Buffalo, WY 82834
www.wordcrafts.net

ACKNOWLEDGEMENTS

In 2014, I had the privilege to teach an in-depth study from the Book of Revelation. The class seemed to really enjoy what we were learning. They encouraged me to take the lectures from this class and turn them into a book. After time spent in prayer, I felt I should. This book, which is a compilation of my lecture notes along with some "extra digging," is the result. I want to thank my class for all of the encouragement they gave me. You know who you are and this book is dedicated to you. You all are the best.

I would also like to thank my husband, Steve. Without his advice, wisdom and support, I never would have even tried. Thank you honey, I love you so very much.

To our children, (who are not children anymore), Kayce and Jennah. You both have been encouraging and so patient with me. Thank you for your love and support. I love you both so much.

To my publishers, Mike and Paula Parker at Wordcrafts Press, for taking a chance on me; and to David Warren for all of your help and talent with imagery.

And last, but certainly not least, I humbly lift up my Lord and Savior Jesus Christ. He put this urgency in my spirit years ago, guided my pen along the way through all of the lectures that were prepared, and opened a door for me to teach this important message. I give Him honor and praise for all of His love and guidance over me. Without Him, nothing is possible.

In Memoriam

In loving memory of my brother, Keith James Bradley - who was proud of me.

BEFORE YOU READ
THIS BOOK

Since this is a study *guide* and not an actual Bible study, I thought I should share the reasons why I wrote this book.

Many years ago I was part of a Bible study on the book of Revelation. As we dug deep into the book's mysteries, I realized that even though it has all of the warnings, the plagues, the judgments, etc., it is really a book of how much God loves us, and to what lengths He will go to save us. As I saw clearly that He loves us and does not want anyone to perish, I fell deeper in love with God. I have had a desire to teach from this viewpoint ever since.

Many people avoid the book of Revelation because of all of its judgments and darkness, and let's be honest - it's also hard to understand. Now, let me be very clear here; I am not a Bible scholar and I am not an expert on this subject. I'm actually a pretty simple person, so I approach Revelation in a simple way. I give a historic overview of what the times were like when John was writing his book, then pull from differing commentaries to give you a broader viewpoint.

I could have gone deeper and cross referenced 1,000 times more than I did. But if I had cross referenced every bit of scripture, this book would be as thick as "War and Peace." Instead, I hope to give you information that will further your understanding before you dig deeper into a study of this complicated book. I am not here to sway your view on how to believe, or to push a particular theological point of view on you. That is between you and the Holy Spirit.

This is a study companion to deepen your understanding of the subject matter, and help you realize as I did, just how much your Father God loves you.

My heart for you is to pay attention. The climate is changing in our world and we need to be prepared of what may come. There are plenty of great books on this subject to read on this. But know the Word and what it says first, before you step out into conspiracy theories and get lost and confused. As you read, consider God's sovereignty over rulers and nations. Ask Him to show you His hand in current world events. Then consider His sovereignty over events in your life. Trust Him to work through these events to accomplish His good purposes for the world, and for you.

With that said, thank you for taking the time to read this companion study, and may you be blessed in your understanding of God's Holy Word.

Note: I want to point out when I talk about satan or the anti-christ I will not capitalize their names. They get no glory from me, even in matters of grammar and punctuation.

This!

CONTENTS

Author's Note: I recommend you first read the chapter in Revelation and then read the corresponding chapter in this book. Taking it chapter by chapter will help further your understanding of this deep and mysterious book.

INTRODUCTION

REVELATION 1:1-10

Have you read or seen *The Lord of the Rings?*

> *"When Aragorn arose all that beheld him gazed in silence, for it seemed to them that he was revealed to them now for the first time. Tall as the sea-kings of old, he stood above all that were near; ancient of days he seemed and yet in the flower of manhood; and wisdom sat upon his brow, and strength and healing were in his hands, and a light was about him. And then Faramir cried: "Behold the King."*

J.R.R. Tolkien, Lord of the Rings

J.R.R. Tolkien knew that human history is all about the *real* battle between good and evil. He knew that the true King has not yet been revealed in His splendor, but will one day.

This is what Revelation is about.

An Unveiling

The word, "Revelation," in Greek is: "apokalupsis" *(ap-ok-al'-oop-sis): to uncover something which is hidden an unveiling or disclosure.* It's where we get the word "Apocalypse" from.

The message of Revelation is called a prophecy, which means we should think of it as a "forth telling" (direction) and a "fore-telling (prediction) of God's will. It's a book about love - the love God has for His children and His desire to not see any perish.

We will learn about the visions that God allowed the book's author, the

Apostle John, to see and then pass on to the first century Church, and to seven specific local churches. My hope is that after reading this, you will realize that God is in control of it all; that He is always in control. This is all a part of His great and mighty plan. Nothing that has happened, or will happen, is out of His sight or His reach. It is all part of a plan that was set in place at the beginning. He loves you and desires for you to have a relationship with Him. He does not want you to perish in eternal hell (yes, there is an eternal hell).

Then there's Jesus Christ - God's only son - who died for our sins. He will defeat the enemy of God, and He will prevail. These are the solid themes that ring throughout the Bible. I call it the Scarlet Cord of Love.

I want you to understand the real hope we have in Jesus. For people who have no faith, listening to today's news would seem like we are spinning helplessly out of control. As believers in Jesus Christ, we know (because the Bible tells us so), that things *will* get worse; but out of control? Hopeless? No.

Hint: I've read the end of the book and we win! *AMEN!*

A Book of Hope

The book of Revelation should be a book of hope for us. Too many of us don't think of it that way because we think of it as a book of hell fire and brimstone. There are warnings, yes, but it's also a book of victory - the victory of the King of kings and the Lord of lords: Jesus Christ, the Son of God.

Failing to read this book is like reading a great novel and ignoring the final chapter. God has an incredible final chapter for this world. And, there is a blessing that awaits all who read it too.

> *"Blessed is the one who reads the words of this prophecy, and blessed are those who hear it and take to heart what is written in it, because the time is near."*

Revelation 1:3

Revelation is the culmination of God's plan. The devil, the dragon, the great destroyer are all players, but they are ultimately defeated by God's Son. In Revelation:

- Sin is finally destroyed.
- God and man walk together in a garden with a tree of life and

the river of life among them, (as God had laid out in His original plan).

- The Story comes to its completion.

How could any child of God not want to know this story?

The Foundation

The book of Revelation was written by John to seven churches in Asia that were undergoing persecution by the emperor of Rome. Most commentaries believe it was either the emperor Nero, or Domitian.

Let's get a foundation of history first and make some key points here before moving on. Wherever *Asia Minor* is mentioned in the New Testament, it refers to the Roman province occupying a region that we know today as modern Turkey.

During the period of Greek dominance, the kings of Pergamum controlled the region. In 133 B.C., the Roman republic expanded and the senate of Rome assumed control making Asia a province. As Rome developed from a republic to an empire, several cities built temples in honor of the various emperors. The growing popularity of emperor worship became a serious threat to the Asian Christians by the time Revelation was written.[1]

For example:

Domitian:

The Roman emperor Domitian called himself "savior" and "lord," claiming divine worship from the Roman citizens. He hated Christians, whose worship of Jesus used the same words, so he persecuted them.[2]

Nero:

This emperor had his victims killed in horrible ways. Some were torn apart by vicious dogs, others were crucified and still others were turned into living torches (*yes, burned alive*), all in a circus-like atmosphere.[3] Apparently though, there is belief that Domitian was even worse than Nero.

Our Author

John is a prisoner of Rome, and he is exiled on the island of Patmos about 30-50 miles off the coast of Asia Minor. He is visited by an angel, given visions of the future and instructed to send what was revealed to seven churches in Asia Minor (remember, this is a region occupied by the Roman Empire). He is there because of *"the Word of God and the testimony of Jesus."* Christians were being persecuted for their faith and he was writing to his fellow believers who were suffering for these reasons.

As we read and study this Revelation together, I want us to remember Who is, Who *always* is, in control - no matter what it looks like around us. God Almighty is on the Throne and He is in complete control of it all.

Psalm 46 is a great reminder for us.

> *God is our refuge and strength,*
> *an ever-present help in trouble.*
> *Therefore we will not fear, though the earth give way*
> *and the mountains fall into the heart of the sea,*
> *though its waters roar and foam*
> *and the mountains quake with their surging.*
> *There is a river whose streams make glad the city of God,*
> *the holy place where the Most High dwells.*
> *God is within her, she will not fall;*
> *God will help her at break of day.*
> *Nations are in uproar, kingdoms fall;*
> *he lifts his voice, the earth melts.*
> *The Lord Almighty is with us;*
> *the God of Jacob is our fortress.*
> *Come and see what the Lord has done,*
> *the desolations he has brought on the earth.*
> *He makes wars cease*
> *to the ends of the earth.*
> *He breaks the bow and shatters the spear;*
> *he burns the shields with fire.*
> *He says, "Be still, and know that I am God;*
> *I will be exalted among the nations,*
> *I will be exalted in the earth."*
> *The Lord Almighty is with us;*
> *the God of Jacob is our fortress.*

Jesus is Savior and Lord and He is coming again.

The Great Debates

There are many interpretations of Revelation, so how do we handle the tough issues of this book? Answer: With prayer and great care.

Here's why. God says;

> *"I warn everyone who hears the words of the prophecy of this book: If anyone adds anything to them, God will add to him the plagues described in this book. And if anyone takes words away from this book of prophecy, God will take away from him his share in the tree of life and in the Holy City, which are described in this book."*
>
> Revelation 22:18-19

Most of the arguments over this book (in my opinion) are about *time*. When will this happen? When will that happen? Then all the chatter starts with: are you pre-tribulation or post-tribulation? Do you believe the *Amillennialism* viewpoint? Or the *Postmilleniam* viewpoint? Are you *Historic premillennial* or *Dispensational premillenial?*

A person can get lost with all of this!

I don't even know what half of it means, and personally, I don't think it is truly important to the big picture. It takes our eyes off of Christ. I don't relish the debate over these things. Some people do and that is good for them I suppose - as long as they don't take their eyes off of Christ.

Sadly though, when I listen to the debates about all of this, that is exactly what happens. I have found that when you go on these rabbit trails of speculation, end time novels and things of that nature, those viewpoints usually become dividing tools in discussions, and isn't that exactly what the enemy wants?

As we read on, I will work at avoiding those types of speculations. My goal is to do my best to focus on what the Word of God says. The Bible is living and active. Ask the Lord to show you more. He will.

For instance:

> *"When Professor Stuart, one of the greatest biblical authorities, was asked one time by his scholars to explain this book to them, he told them he wouldn't 'till he understood it. Now, if you wait 'till you understand every stone, tree, bush and blade of grass in a picture it will be a long time before you admire it. And so with our food. If you wait to analyze every kind of edible thing on the table it will be a long while indeed before you enjoy it. Just because we*

can't understand every thought, word, and picture in the Book of Revelation - is no reason why we should not give our attention to what we can understand in it."[4]

H. A. Buttz

Stay close to His Word and what He says in it; not someone's interpretation of it. The book of Revelation both opens and closes with promises of blessings to those who *heed* its teachings (Revelation 1:3 & 22:7) – not to those who intellectually decipher its prophetic language.

The Story of a Coin

There is an ancient legend of a king who had a terrified army. They had a strong enemy with a high fortress and mighty weapons. The king was confident in victory, but he wondered how he would convince his army.

After thinking about it, he decided to tell them he had a prophetic coin that predicted the outcome of battles. If the coin landed on the eagle side, they would win. If it landed on the bear side, they would lose.

The army gathered around, the coin was tossed and landed on the eagle side. They all shouted, "We will win!" The army marched against their enemy and won. It was only later that the king revealed that it was a two sided coin with eagles on both sides.

That fictional story contains a reliable truth: *"An assured victory empowers an army."*[5]

We are assured a victory as well. There is hope, whether it is to keep on marching or keep on waiting.

Christ *will* prevail.

AMEN!

Endnotes:

1. Kendall Easely, Revelation- Holman New Testament Commentary 1998 B & H Publishing Group; Nashville,TN; pg 25
2. Ibid., pg 17
3. Community Bible Study TD Helps; 2008; Lesson 1; pg 2
4. http://Biblehub.com/sermons/auth/buttz/prophecy_though_difficult_to_ understand_must_yet_be_studied.htm
5. Community Bible Study TD Helps; 2008; Lesson 1; pg 3

CHAPTER 1

Do you have many keys? I do. I have keys to my car, house, church, office, my husband's car, our son's car and our daughter's car as well; not to mention keys to homes of friends and neighbor.

When you think about it, a key symbolizes *power*.

For those locked out, a key means access - because the person holding the key is no longer an outsider. But for those locked in, a key can mean freedom.

Whether you are locked in or locked out, the one holding the key is the one holding the power.[1]

Who Holds The Key

John is in exile. He is locked away as a prisoner of Rome, but he understands who holds the keys. Jesus holds the keys. I want us to remember that: No matter what life looks like around us, Jesus holds the keys.

Revelation 1:10 starts with, *"On the Lord's day..."* By John's time, the "Lord's day" was the Christian's first day of the week - our Sunday - in honor of Jesus' resurrection.

He (John) was *in the Spirit*. This marks the beginning of four major visions that are revealed, and he was told to write down everything he saw.

Psychologists tell us we remember far more of what we see than of what we hear or read. It's true. For example, children learn better when shown through actions or through pictures than just being given instructions. This may be why God is using vivid images with symbolism to help us grasp and remember this divine message.

The Seven Churches

John is told to write down what he sees on a scroll and send it to seven churches located in the ancient cities of Ephesus, Smyrna, Pergamum, Thyatira, Sardis, Philadelphia and Laodicea.

Some scholars believe this is because the cities were mail distribution centers for the region, making it easier for the book to spread to other places and to other churches. The cities were roughly thirty to fifty miles apart along a circular road. The book of Revelation lists them in the sequence a letter carrier would travel, arriving by ship from Patmos (where John was) to Ephesus (then clockwise from Ephesus): north to Smyrna and Pergamum; east to Thyatira; south to Sardis; southeast to Philadelphia and Laodicea; west back to Ephesus. This is referred to as the Circular Road.

Referring to verse 12 and the lampstands, it is believed the seven golden lampstands were possibly a seven-branched candelabrum - as the one placed in the Israelite tabernacle of the Old Testament.

> "Their bulbs and their branches shall be of one piece with it; all of it shall be one piece of hammered work of pure gold. Then you shall make its lamps seven in number; and they shall mount its lamps so as to shed light on the space in front of it. Its snuffers and their trays shall be of pure gold. "It shall be made from a talent of pure gold, with all these utensils. See that you make them after the pattern for them, which was shown to you on the mountain."
>
> Exodus 25:36-40

In Zechariah, his vision of a lampstand represented Israel also.

> "He asked me, 'What do you see?' I answered, 'I see a solid gold lampstand with a bowl at the top and seven lamps on it, with seven channels to the lamps.'"
>
> Zechariah 4:2

It is safe to say that in this vision, the lampstand represents each of the Christian churches mentioned - God's new people. John writes in 1:13 that he sees someone "like the son of man." In John's Gospel, he records Jesus often referring to Himself as "Son of Man." In fact, the "Son of Man" is Jesus' own self-description - he uses the title 12 times in the Gospel of John (1:51; 3:13-14; 5:27; 6:27, 53, 62; 8:28; 9:35; 12:23; 13:31).

We read about this in a vision Daniel had too:

*"In my vision at night I looked, and there before me was one like a **son of man**, coming with the clouds of heaven. He approached the Ancient of Days and was led into his presence."*

Daniel 7:13

This must be Jesus - our Savior, glorious and powerful beyond measure.

Our High Priest

John goes on to describe Him in dress as the high priest that He is, with *"A robe reaching down to His feet and with a golden sash around His chest"* (1:13). The high priests of the Old Testament wore full-length robes with sashes. The reference to Christ as the high priest is supported by the reference to the golden sash around His waist. This links Him in His appearance with the high priest of Israel. I encourage you to read more about the garments the priests wore in Exodus, chapter 39.

Verse 14 goes on to say, *"His head and hair were white like wool, as white as snow."* This represents pure wisdom and dignity. Long ago, white hair symbolized the respect due to the aged person for the wisdom of their advanced years. Proverbs 16:31 says, *"Gray hair is a crown of splendor; it is attained in the way of righteousness."* Christ is righteous.

"His eyes were blazing like fire..." They see all. He has much insight to see into the heart of man, and sees through the heart as well. Verse 15 says *"His feet were like bronze glowing in a furnace..."* In the introduction to one of the great Psalms about the coming of the Messiah, King David writes:

"The LORD says to my lord: Sit at my right hand until I make your enemies a footstool for your feet."

Psalm 110: 1

The picture is of a powerful King who has subdued his enemies to the point that they are nothing more than a king's footstool. Some ancient kings symbolized their victories by literally placing their feet on the necks of defeated enemies. In the book of Joshua that is exactly what Joshua commanded his commanders to do:

"When they had brought these kings to Joshua, he summoned all the men of Israel and said to the army commanders who had come with him, 'Come here and put your feet on the necks of these kings.' So they came forward and placed their feet on their necks."

Joshua 10:24

How intimidating. How demoralizing for the defeated one. Now picture the powerful bronze glowing feet of Jesus on the neck of the enemy. This is the ultimate triumph over all the forces of evil. What a picture!

Out of His Mouth

He has a voice of powerful rushing water. In verse 10 we read that Jesus had a voice like a trumpet and now His voice is like rushing water. Have you heard the power and volume of a trumpet blast? Or have you ever been near a dam or a large water fall? Think about Niagara Falls. Powerful! Whether referencing the trumpet or the sound of rushing water, both cannot and will not be ignored.

Verse 16 goes on to say that John see's Jesus holding seven stars in His right hand. If you read this chapter of Revelation, you already know that later, in Verse 20, Jesus says the lampstands are the churches and the stars are the angels.

The Greek word here for angel is *angelos*, which means *messenger* - either human or divine. In this case, the "angel" means the "messenger" for the church. This could mean a guardian angel, or it could be interpreted as the Pastors or Ministers of a church, or any believer in a leadership role of any kind. These are the ones that shepherd His sheep. Because they're in His hands, they are under His protection and His care (*more about that later*).

Verse 16 continues with Christ's description and says *"out of His mouth came a sharp double edged sword."* In Hebrews the voice of truth is referred to as a double edged sword.

> *"For the word of God is alive and active. Sharper than any double-edged sword, it penetrates even to dividing soul and spirit, joints and marrow; it judges the thoughts and attitudes of the heart."*
>
> Hebrews 4:12

Jesus only speaks truth.

This is a sword, not a dagger. Swords are used more for battle than daggers. Revelation 19:15 says, *"Out of His mouth comes a sharp sword with which to strike down the nations."* The sword stands for the power to conquer His enemies and protect His people. Because Jesus speaks truth, He has the power and authority to judge, too. He speaks *only* truth. There is comfort in that.

Like The Sun Shining

His face displays the glory of God, *"like the sun shining in all its brilliance."* 1:16

John is looking into the face of Jesus. He saw Jesus on the Mount of Transfiguration as well.

> *"There He was transfigured before them. His face shone like the sun, and His clothes became as white as the light."*
>
> Matthew 17:2

Imagine if you had seen this image yourself? If I had seen that, I would have fallen to the floor in terror - as if dead, just like John said he did. But soon, I'm sure that feeling (once I got past the terror) would turn to an overwhelming reverence for Him, and there would be such a desire to just worship Him, just like Joshua and Gideon did.

The Jesus that John saw both on the Mount of Transfiguration and on the island of Patmos, is none other than Almighty God!

Jesus says in verse 17 that He is the *"First and the Last, Living One."* He has said this before too.

> *"Just as the living Father sent me and I live because of the Father, so the one who feeds on me will live because of me."*
>
> John 6:57

He holds the keys to Death and Hades. This duo is limited in their power by Jesus - who is the key *holder*. We need to remember that all of these demons, and yes, even satan himself, are created beings. We tend to put this enemy on the same level as God, and he simply is not.

Our enemy, satan is a created being. He was created by God, who is not a created being - He is **the Creator**. I heard this perspective from a very wise pastor named Bill Johnson who resides over Bethel Church in Redding, California. Here's what he had to say in his book, *Hosting the Presence:*

> *"Never at any time has satan been a threat to God. God is ultimate in power and might, beauty and glory...ever at any time has satan been a threat to God. The entire realm of darkness could be forever wiped out with a word. But God chose to defeat him through those made in His own likeness—those who would*

worship God by choice. Brilliant. It was the issue of worship that brought about his rebellion in the first place."[2]

That transformed my perspective. I hope it does yours as we study this book of Revelation.

Author Kendall Easley said, *"Jesus lives to pray for us just as he died to save us. Because He has unending life, He has the power to extend eternal life to all who trust in Him."*[3] If we approach life from the victorious side and know Christ as holy, power and love, then trust me, life's challenges will be much easier to take.

Transform your focus on Christ and His love for you and His power and strength. Not on the prince of this world. This adversary of God is just not worth your time and energy. Period.

The Lampstands

John is told to write what he has seen; what is now, and what will take place later. Then Jesus reveals the mystery of the lampstands and stars.

As I said earlier, *angel* mean *messenger*, which means *our* messenger. And the messengers of our day could be our pastors. But it can also mean anyone who brings the Word of God to a brother or sister. I'm not talking about just a formal church setting, or Bible study, or conference or author, etc.

It could mean encouraging one another over the phone, or over coffee, or a mother or father who's out with the kids that day. What I'm trying to say is that we are all messengers of Christ. Why? Because of His testimony. If we have accepted Jesus Christ into our hearts then He lives there inside of us and we reflect His glory. Matthew says;

> *"You are the light of the world. A city set on a hill cannot be hidden; nor does anyone light a lamp and put it under a basket, but on the lampstand, and it gives light to all who are in the house. Let your light shine before men in such a way that they may see your good works, and glorify your Father who is in heaven."*
>
> Matthew 5:14-16

We are the light bearers of Christ, and if we are His light bearers, then we are His messengers as well, so know what His Word says. Get to know the character of God through His Word. He loves you and wants you near Him.

Our Testimony

In John's day, the church was in trouble because of the Word of God and the testimony of Jesus. The church in our day is in trouble for the same thing with one exception: they were in trouble for proclaiming the Word of God and we are in trouble for *not* proclaiming it.

Too often we overlook obvious biblical truths for fear of hurting feelings. Too many times we separate ourselves and our children from the unbelieving world, instead of looking at it as fertile ground for the Word of God. We bless each other, but don't go after the lost.

"What would they think of me?" "What would they say?" "They would think I am weird."

We as Christians of today, often live in our own self-imposed exile for fear of rejection and it seems we are more concerned about others opinion of us than God's opinion of us. If we are to live our lives through Jesus Christ our Lord, our risen Savior, then we too are key holders to freedom - our own freedom and someone else's.

This is our ministry in a nutshell: to be the light in a dark world and unlock the doors of imprisonment with truth. The truth will set you free! The truth is knowing who Jesus Christ is and He is love.

Endnotes:

1. Ibid., Lesson 2; pg 5
2. Bill Johnson, Hosting His Presence, Destiny Image Publishers, Inc. 2012, pg.34
3. Kendall Easely, Revelation- Holman New Testament Commentary 1998 B & H Publishing Group; Nashville,TN; pg 20

CHAPTER 2

A boy went off to college and at the end of the first semester, he began to panic. He had planned to study, really he had - but college life was something to be experienced - and he did. It was so much fun! But, there was no escaping the consequences. He had to tell his parents the truth. So he emailed his mother:

> *"Coming home. Failed everything. Please prepare Dad.*
>
> *Love, John."*

In a few days, he received a response from his mom. It read:

> *"Dad is prepared. Please prepare yourself.*
>
> *Love, Mom."*[1]

In this chapter, Jesus is alerting these churches to get prepared, because He is coming.

The *Church* of Jesus Christ is made up of the *people* of Jesus Christ. And the bottom line is that we need to be prepared. Jesus *is* coming back.

My sister was a banker for many years. She told me how bank workers are trained to spot counterfeit money. They don't study all the different counterfeits (there are just too many of them). Instead, they study the "real deal" - the authentic bills. That way, when a counterfeit shows up, they will recognize it. They prepared themselves so much to recognize the real one, that the false one stands out like a sore thumb!

This is what Jesus is saying here. *Know Me. And by knowing Me you'll be preparing yourselves for My return.* Jesus was walking among them - the churches/lampstands - and He is observing their deeds and motives, like a shepherd to the sheep, overlooking and inspecting His flock. There are compliments and encouragements, but also constructive criticisms. It's the same with us too. Jesus wants us to grow in Him, but He also wants us to be prepared for His coming, and He uses these churches as examples for us to learn by.

To help us better understand Jesus' words, let's look at the culture and the church life of the day in each of these cities.

About the city of Ephesus: Busy

Why would Jesus say that they *"have forsaken their first love"* in 2:4?

By the time John wrote Revelation, Ephesus had been an important seaport city for over 1,000 years. It had been ruled by both the Persians and Greeks before coming under Roman rule in 133 B.C. It was the fourth largest city in the Roman world. Rome was the first, then the city of Alexandria, then Antioch, and then Ephesus, which was inhabited by about 300,000 people. That's a decent sized city. I live in the Nashville Tennessee area, and as of the date of this book, the population of Nashville is currently around 600,000. That should give you an idea of how big Ephesus was.

During John's time, Ephesus was truly splendid. A broad street lined with columns led east from the harbor to the city amphitheater, which seated approximately 25,000 people. It featured numerous finely sculpted temples, the most magnificent of all being the temple to Artemis, the local fertility goddess. This structure was approximately 400 ft. long x 200 ft. wide. It had 127 columns that were each 60 ft. high, all made of marble. It took up more space than a football field.[2]

Just think about that for a moment. The temple of Artemis was huge! That must have been spectacular to see. On the down side, the city was also known for dealing in slavery, prostitution and idol worship.

In Ephesus, a large Jewish population thrived and Christianity was fully established with the two-year ministry of Paul during his third missionary journey (if you want to read about Paul's journey there, it's found in Acts 19). The gospel was so successful, that devotion to the Greek goddess Artemis was threatened.

The Church of Ephesus: Busy

There was a heretical sect within the church called the Nicolaitans. They had worked out a compromise with the pagan society which was threatened by the rapid growth of Christianity. There was now open practices of sexual immorality (perhaps at the pagan temple because she was the fertility god), and open participation in eating food that had been sacrificed to idols. These practices could be interpreted as "duties" of the loyal Ephesian citizen.[3]

The Ephesian Church worked hard at counteracting the Nicolaitans and their wicked practices. This was the same church that received the Holy Spirit and that spoke in tongues and prophesied (see Acts 19:6). Maybe this is why Paul was motivated to write this passage in Ephesians. He saw the compromise in this sect and wanted to encourage them.

> *"For our struggle is not against flesh and blood, but against the rulers, against the authorities, against the powers of this dark world and against the spiritual forces of evil in the heavenly realms."*
>
> Ephesians 6:12

The Ephesian Church worked hard and did not tolerate wickedness. They tested the teachings that circulated and persevered and had not grown weary in their well doing. This is a good thing, right? Yes. However, in their pursuit of truth and their patience in persecution, these Christians had allowed a tragic flaw to infect their fellowship. Jesus said:

> *"You have forsaken your first love."*
>
> Revelation 2:4

They became a loveless church.

In rooting out the error and expelling false teachers, they had grown suspicious of one another. Their good deeds were now motivated by duty rather than love.

Jesus follows with a strong warning in the very next verse.

> *"If you do not repent, I will come and remove your lampstand from its place."*
>
> Revelation 2:5

I have been a part of a closing of a church. I remember it well. My husband and I had moved to town and were looking for a church home. We found a small church with a new young pastor that had inherited his role at this established church. We loved his teaching, and became friends with him and his family too, so we stayed for a bit.

Over time, we couldn't put our finger on it, but we knew something was terribly wrong. Things just felt "off." Then one Sunday morning our pastor made a very hard decision and spoke to the congregation with a somber tone and ended his speech to us with, "Therefore, this church cannot go on any longer, so I am closing its doors forever."

You see, there was no love or unity within it anymore. Apparently, before this pastor came to take over, church members would argue over everything, from theology to what to wear, and they became suspicious of one another. He tried to revive this hurting church, but the people would have none of it. They were stiff necked and prideful. He had no choice but to close its doors. It was truly like suffering a death. I'll never forget it. But he did the right thing.

A loveless church is no longer a church. It bears no fruit. It was hard to watch, but we knew our pastor sought the Lord for guidance. We stood with him in decision and moved on to another church. You see, Christ has the right, as ruler and sovereign judge to extinguish such a congregation.

Tragically, the Ephesian church, who was praised by Paul earlier in its day, ultimately did not repent for the loveless state it was in, and eventually succumbed to the pagan ways that surrounded them. Today, neither their city nor the church exist…their lampstand was removed just as Christ had warned.

Let me ask you something. What motivates you in your service to Him? Is it love? Or are you just holding people to rules and regulations?

1 Corinthians 13:13 says, *"And now these three remain: faith, hope and love. But the greatest of these is love."*

John 13:35 says, *"By this everyone will know that you are my disciples, if you love one another."*

Without love, we are nothing. If you find yourself forsaking your first love, then look to the cross of Jesus. What Jesus did out of love on the cross, He did for you. He did for all of us.

The bottom line is, if we look to the cross then we will recover our first love. You can count on that. What's that old song by Peter Scholtes we used to sing? *"And they'll know we are Christians by our love, by our love, yes they'll know we are Christians by our love…"*⁴

About the city of Smyrna:

Jesus wants them to stay faithful in persecution.

The city of Smyrna was located at the site of the present day city of

Izmir, Turkey. It was about 35 miles north of Ephesus and had approximately 200,000 people residing there. It was a wealthy city, known for its science, medicine and architecture. Smyrna was also considered the safest seaport of its time. It had a thriving economy because it was on the main trade route from Rome to India and Persia. Alexander the Great personally planned the city, and it was called *the ornament of Asia* because of its beauty and splendor. Many Jews lived there, yet Smyrna was overwhelmingly pagan.[5] On one end of the main street, the "street of gold," stood the Temple of Zeus, and at the other end stood the Temple of Cybele, "the mother of the gods." Smyrna was the center of emperor worship in the Roman Empire, boasting a temple to Tiberius Caesar.[6] To honor Cybele, the pagan priests were castrated and called "third gender."[7]

Church of Smyrna *suffering*

There was also a large Jewish population who opposed Christianity, and followed Rome's pagan ways. This may be why Jesus refers to Smyrna as *"a synagogue of satan"* in 2:9.

The people of Smyrna had long been known for their extreme loyalty to Rome. But the gospel came because of Paul's third missionary journey there, and it had taken root. (Acts 19:10)

A little history note:

Polycarp, the Bishop of Smyrna, was one of the first officials of the church to be arrested for his faithful stance as a Christian. He was killed/martyred for not renouncing Jesus Christ as his Savior. He is quoted as saying:

> *"Eighty-six years I have served him, and he never did me any wrong. How can I blaspheme my King who saved me?"*[8]

Are you getting an idea as to why Jesus came to encourage them to hold on? Smyrna, as a city, was hostile and oppressive against Christians. The church of Smyrna was the only church besides the church of Philadelphia to *not* be criticized by Christ. Jesus is saying to the church of Smyrna, *hang on and stay faithful.*

A long time ago, I thought persecution happened only in faraway places; not in my country. Now there's been a time of church burnings, young Christians singled out and shot at schools, and shooters killing Christians during church services. Our government has legislated hate-crime laws, but have you ever noticed that when Christians are killed, it is not called a hate-crime? In many instances our government has also made it illegal for Christians to practice their faith outwardly in public.

Just recently I heard about two women who lost their jobs for practicing their faith. One was school related and one was in the mental health field. They lost their jobs for practicing what they believe as Christ followers.

Such subtle persecutions are the work of the devil, who wants to destroy our Christian witness. The devil has been persecuting Christians from the beginning. Persecution is not just in other countries as we see in the news; it's here, there and everywhere. It is happening everyday.

It all started off subtle but it is gaining speed. Just like it did in Smyrna. The question is, are we prepared? Will we stay the course for Christ?

Let's move on to the churches of Pergamum and Thyatira. They were warned not to practice false doctrine.

About the city of Pergamum

Located about 55 miles north of Smyrna, Pergamum was built on the slope of a hill rising almost 1,000 ft. above the surrounding plain. This provides not only a breathtaking view, but military security as well. The name *Pergamum* means *citadel* in Greek. Its location is where Bergama, Turkey is today.

Pergamum had temples built for Zeus, Caesar and the goddess Athena, who were the pagan deities that was worshipped there. The temple for Zeus stood at the top of the hill and had an altar dedicated to him that was 120 ft. x 112 ft.[9] That's huge!

Jesus praises the believers who remain true to Him in this hostile territory that Jesus remarks as the place *"where satan dwells"* (2:13).

The Church of Pergamum   confused

The church of Pergamum apparently had the opposite problem of the Ephesian church. Rather than testing and rejecting false teachers, they had accepted people who held to the teachings of Balaam. Idolatry and immorality were seeping into their doctrine. Pergamum had another problem: the Nicolaitans, (the heretical sect of the church I mentioned earlier), were also here. You see, this church tolerated two heretical movements.

1. Some compromised with *"the teaching of Balaam"* (2:14). They assist God's people in sinning by eating meat sacrificed to idols and by committing sexual sins.
2. Others compromised by holding to this Nicolaitan heresy and helping Christians rationalize sinful behavior in some fashion.[10]

Jesus speaks plainly in 2:14.

> *"Nevertheless, I have a few things against you: You have people there who hold to the teaching of Balaam, who taught Balak to entice the Israelites to sin by eating food sacrificed to idols and by committing sexual immorality."*

The book of Numbers, chapters 22-24 tells the story in detail of how the false prophet and king at first seemed to fail in the direct attempts to curse Israel. Later, however, they (The Moabites) did succeed in leading the people of God astray indirectly, by idolatry and immorality. Jesus goes on to say,

> *"Likewise you also have those who hold to the teaching of the Nicolaitans. Repent therefore. Otherwise, I will soon come to you and will fight against them with the sword of my mouth."*
>
> Revelation 2:15-16

This is pretty direct language from Christ. Yet He speaks with such encouragement to the ones who overcome in the very next verse.

> *"To him who overcomes, I will give some of the hidden manna. I will also give him a white stone with a new name written on it, known only to him who receives it."*
>
> Revelation 2:17

It is possible that the *hidden manna* refers to some sort of future divine nourishment, and the *white stone* could represent a symbol of victory, or a pardon from a death sentence.

And as for the new name mentioned, God often gave people a new name at a turning point in their lives. For example: Abram became Abraham; Jacob became Israel; Simon became Peter, etc. So it will be for the overcomers and conquerors in the kingdom. Moral of this story - don't compromise and you'll be rewarded.

About the city of Thyatira

Thyatira was located about half way between Pergamum and Sardis, approximately 20 miles Southeast of Pergamum. It had served as a military outpost for the kingdom of Pergamum and came under Roman rule at the same time as Pergamum, which was in 133 B.C. It was located in a valley and also had many trading posts. Today it is known as Akhisar, Turkey. They were known for their many trade guilds, particularly among the coppersmiths, fabric weavers and dyers of material.

The church of Thyatira   tolerant

Among the letters are sent out to the churches, this is the longest, yet Thyatira is the smallest of the seven cities. Sadly, eating meat sacrificed to idols and sexual sins were prevalent. The pagan god Apollo was the primary deity worshipped by this city.

When Christ addresses Thyatira, He refers to Himself as *"the Son of God."* His eyes...*like flames of fire,* can gaze into all matters. His feet...*like burnished bronze,* can trample whatever displeases Him. He praises them for service and perseverance, but there are problems here. Some Christians had adopted the teachings of "Jezebel" as a way to reconcile membership in a trade guild with membership in Christ's church.[11]

The churches of Pergamum and Thyatira had strengths. When persecuted, they did not renounce Jesus. But they were being invaded by modern day culture and began to compromise truth in favor of lies. Sound familiar?

Let's talk about what Christ meant when He mentioned that they tolerate this "Jezebel" in 2:20. She is the reason why Christians stumble. Christ is gracious and loving, and He has allowed her time to repent, but she refuses (2:21). Because He is also just, He announces judgment upon her, and all who join themselves with her will also suffer in this judgment.

Let's talk about Jezebel for a moment. This could be a person *or a spirit* - scripture is not clear on this point. However, there is a "Jezebel spirit" that does exist among some people, so let's look at her story.

The story is found in 1 Kings 18:17-40. She dominated her husband in religious matters and her great opponent was the prophet Elijah, who triumphed over the priests of Baal at Mt. Carmel. She had great power as the queen-mother but she met with a violent death. That was God's verdict on her life (2 Kings 9:30-37).

Because of her vicious rejection of Yahweh, Israel's true God, her name became a byword for evil and religious apostasy. It still exists today.

Here in Revelation, is the only time her name appears in the New Testament and it is "code" for *false prophetess*.

Our risen Christ fully knows all the strengths and weaknesses of each of the congregations. The church is Christ's. It belongs to Him, and He holds it accountable to Himself.

Each of the seven letters begins with "I know." The Greek word for this is *oida*. Oida basically means *factual knowledge*.[12]

Regarding Ephesus, 2:2 Jesus says,

> *"I know your deeds, your hard work…"*

Addressing Smyrna in 2:9 He says,

> *"I know your afflictions and poverty…"*

With Pergamum He says in 2:13,

> *"I know where you live - where satan has his throne."*

And with Thyatira He says in 2:19,

> *"I know your deeds, your love and faith…yet you tolerate that woman Jezebel…"*

Each of the four churches in this chapter have characteristics not found in the others and Christ is fully aware of them all - even 2,000 years later He is aware of *all* His churches' characteristics.

If Jesus showed up to our church today, what compliments would He give us? What criticisms would He make? What would He *know* about us? Would He have a good opinion of us?

Going back to the counterfeit money example - how well do we know the truth?

Nowadays, theory is taught as fact and fact is taught as theory. Just look at how evolution is being taught in our schools. It is taught as fact, when in reality it is only theory. Christianity is seen as a theory when in reality it is a fact. Jesus really lived, and He really died, and He really rose from the dead. Jesus is real.

What we believe and how we live *matters to God.* Let's examine our own lives in the light of God's Word. Don't be ensnared by false teachings. This is a chance to be prepared.

> *We are not citizens of earth trying to get to heaven. We are citizens of heaven, trying to get through this world.*
>
> Anonymous

I'll end this chapter with this translation from Romans:

> *"Don't copy the behavior and customs of this world, but let God transform you into a new person by changing the way you think. Then you will learn to know God's will for you, which is good and pleasing and perfect."*
>
> Romans 12:2 (NLT)

Endnotes:

1. Community Bible Study TD Helps; 2008; Lesson 3; pg 8
2. Kendall Easely, Revelation- Holman New Testament Commentary 1998 B & H Publishing Group; Nashville,TN; pg 45
3. Ibid., pg 46
4. 1966, F.E.L. Publications, assigned to The Lorenz Corp., 1991
5. Kendall Easely, Revelation- Holman New Testament Commentary 1998 B & H Publishing Group; Nashville,TN; pg 46
6. http://philologos.org/bpr/files/s008.htm
7. https://en.wikipedia.org/wiki/Cybele
8. http://www.christianity.com/church/church-history/timeline/1-300/polycarp-quote-11629600.html
9. Kendall Easely, Revelation- Holman New Testament Commentary 1998 B & H Publishing Group; Nashville,TN; pg 47
10. Ibid., pg 38
11. Kendall Easely, Revelation- Holman New Testament Commentary 1998 B & H Publishing Group; Nashville,TN; pg 48
12. Ibid., pg 43

CHAPTER 3

Remember when you were in school? After the first six or nine weeks (depending on where you were) came your first progress report for the year. It wasn't your final grade, only an indication of the progress you were making. For some those who studied hard, it was a good evening with the family. There were praises given. For those who shirked their studies, procrastinated and thought nobody knew, it was bad news. It was judgment day. Someone had been watching. You found out that you were not invisible and that there was a record of your progress.[1]

In chapter 3 Jesus continues his "progress report" of the last three churches; Sardis, Philadelphia, Laodicea. Some of the churches are praised and some are rebuked, but Jesus wants to help them be the people He knows they can be - overcomers. He's not just talking to the churches that existed then. He's talking to us today. We are His light in a dark world. He cared about them and He cares about us. Jesus cares about the way we live our lives.

Let's learn about these last three churches and the city and culture they lived in.

About the city of Sardis:

Sardis had a unique geographical location. It was approximately 50 miles inland from the Aegean Sea and 30 miles south of Thyatira. The city lay at the foot of Mount Tmolus that rose 1,500 ft. above the valley of the Hermus River. Because of where it stood, it was a natural citadel.

Before Sardis was captured for the first time, it had been the splendid and wealthy capital of the kingdom of Lydia. Sardis had fallen to the Persians during King Cyrus's reign in 546 B.C., when this citadel was breached in a surprise nighttime attack. Alexander the Great captured the city with the same tactic centuries later, and the city was conquered again by the army of Antiochus III (the Great) using the same exact tactic.

Three times the city fell, and always the same way! Although Sardis never regained its former splendor, by the first century it had a population of approximately 120,000 people within its walls. The old city of Sardis is known today as Sart, Turkey.[2]

The Church of Sardis　DYING

The church of Sardis receives no praise from Christ, only criticism. They had a reputation of being alive, but they were really dead. Christ does not accuse them of heresy, but neither had they offended the Romans or unbelieving Jews either. They had however, offended God by emphasizing formality over the reality. Christ says in 3:2 they must,

> "wake up and strengthen what remains."

He uses a series of verbs in His message to them: *wakeup / strengthen / remember / obey / repent.*[3]

They needed to remember their past. When the Christians at Sardis were converted, they not only received the gospel, but they received the Holy Spirit as well. They were filled with the Holy Spirit and as a result became spiritually alive. But now, they had forgotten about the Spirit's work so they were considered lifeless. On the outside, the church's works and deeds appeared wonderful (this is why they had a reputation of being alive), but Jesus says they are not complete in God's sight. According to the rest of verse two;

> "...for I have not found your deeds complete in the sight of my God."

A reputation is what people think of you, but character is what God knows about you. God knows the heart of man. Christ threatens to judge this lifeless church by coming against them like a thief at an unexpected time if they do not repent (3:3).

Now, just to be clear, some interpreters believe this statement, "like a thief," refers to Christ's second coming, which is often said in the New Testament to be *like a thief.*

I believe in this context the "coming" of the Lord to judge this church is conditional. It will only take place if the church does *not* repent. Jesus says, *"If you do not wake up, I will come like a thief, and you will not know at what time I will come to you."* The second coming of the Lord is *not* conditional. He will come at the appointed time.

Just as the city of Sardis fell to unexpected military attacks, the Church of Sardis will be visited by Christ unexpectedly and be judged if it does not change its attitude and repent.

Are we like the church of Sardis sometimes? Are we more concerned with our reputation than truly having an intimate relationship with Him? Do we want people to think we're "spiritually alive" because of all the things we do at church or for church, but inside we're spiritually dead and we don't really know who Jesus Christ is? Christ was not impressed with Sardis's reputation of being an alive church, a church with a "name," for in reality, when you look at it from God's perspective, it is a dead church - just a hollow shell. If this is your spiritual condition, Jesus encourages you to *"strengthen what remains and is about to die"(3:2b)*. Let the Lord in. Let Him transform and renew your mind. Don't worry so much about your reputation - character is what matters. Even if standing for Him and what is right causes you to lose the approval of the people around you, you will never lose the love of God. Jesus cares about our lives.

Even though there is no praise for this church from Jesus, there are promises to the overcomer, the ones who have not compromised. (Remember, with Christ there is always hope.) They are promised white clothes, symbolizing righteousness. Their name will remain in the book of life - one of the books used by God at the final judgment (more on that when we get to chapter 20). Finally, Jesus says in 3:5 that He *"...will acknowledge his name before the Father and His angels."* All this if we stand firm, overcome, hold true to our faith in Christ and allow the Holy Spirit to dwell in us.

What an honor to be acknowledged in the heavenly kingdom of God. Now that's something to stand for.

About the city of Philadelphia   *Growing*

Because of little archeological work done on this site, there is little known of the exact layout of the ancient city of Philadelphia,.but we do know it was located approximately 30 miles south of Sardis. It was at the head of a fertile plateau, and from this position it had become commercially important. Unfortunately, the area around Philadelphia was an earthquake zone. Today this city is known as Alashehir, Turkey. In A.D. 17 a severe earthquake devastated the city, causing many citizens to leave for a safer place. In the late 1960's another earthquake rocked this area. The region remains geologically unstable.[4]

The Church of Philadelphia

The congregation of Philadelphia was small in members and had *"little strength"* as Christ acknowledges in 3:8, yet He gives them high praise for enduring patiently. What was going on? What were they enduring? In their city, members of the Jewish synagogue had played havoc with the Christians there. These Jews refused to acknowledge Jesus as the Messiah. They claimed to be the *true* people of God, but they were not. Their claim to be Jews was based on their biology only rather than on having the faith that Abraham had demonstrated. They were liars in their rejection of Christ and this is probably why He calls them the *"synagogue of satan"* in 3:9.[5]

There is no text that directly says this, but I think these synagogues might have closed their doors to, or excommunicated these Jewish converts to Jesus. Why would this be such a big deal? Back then, this was their community. Their children grew up together, side by side. They took care of the sick together, they ate together on many occasions, they celebrated and grieved together, etc... These kinds of communities were very close knit, and community was their life source. By excommunicating them, they are shutting them out of their community, isolating them from the social life of the community, cutting off their life source.

Throughout the history of the church, many have suffered for their faith. Some have even died for it. Regardless of details, these Jewish Christians were being unjustly accused or being pressured to compromise their beliefs. God's message to this church is to encourage them. Jesus knows their deeds. They are a committed church and have kept His Word. They have not denied Christ's name. They have patiently endured. Wow. What high praise from the Lord.

In verse 10 Jesus says,

> *"Since you have kept my command to endure patiently, I will also keep you from the hour of trial that is going to come upon the whole world to test those who live on the earth."*

This is the first mention of the "tribulation." The phrase, "keep you from," is Greek and can mean "keep you from undergoing" or literally "keep you from."

The great interpretive challenge regarding this verse is whether Christ is promising to *remove* believers physically *out* of the world before the time of testing, or to *protect* the believers *during* this time. So, what's the answer? I will leave it to you to interpret this scripture for yourself. Let the Holy Spirit teach you. But remember this: whether He *takes* us or *leaves* us, the fact is we will be *with* Christ.

We can do *all* things *through Christ* who will give us our strength (Philippians 4:13). We need to keep our eyes heavenly bound. There is no clear cut answer on this.

Hold on to Jesus and stand firm in your commitment. Like the church of Philadelphia and all that awaits them because of their faithful stand for Jesus, your stand for Christ will become your testimony. And that testimony gives hope to another brother or a sister who is walking in faith in Christ.

About the city of Laodicea

Laodicea is located about 40 miles Southeast of Philadelphia. It was one of the three "sister cities" in the area that included Colossae (which was famous for for its cold springs) and Hierapolis (which was famous for its medicinal hot springs). Being a vital crossroads city made it a major commercial success. During this time Laodicea was a great banking center and had a strong textile industry as well, specializing in black woolen fabrics. It also was famous for its medical school, and was connected with the temple of Asclepius, the Greek god of medicine. The Laodicean physicians were particularly noted for making something called "Phrygian powder." It was described by Aristotle, as a useful cure for eye diseases. Today the location for Laodicea is known as the city of Denizli, Turkey.

The most serious problem with Laodicea was its lack of reliable water. The water was piped in from Colossae, which was miles away. Although Colossae's water was famous for being cool, by the time it reached Laodicea it was lukewarm and tasteless, which made it barely drinkable.[6]

There are lots of people who like hot tea or iced tea, but never lukewarm tea. Why? Because it's tasteless. Imagine that for your drinking water all the time. *Blech.*

The Church of Laodicea Complacent

This church, like her sister church in Sardis, receives no compliment from Christ. They're all problems with no praise. Christ considers them "lukewarm" (making reference to their disgusting lukewarm drinking water). They were considered lukewarm to Him because although they had not totally abandoned the faith, they were not "red hot" in their commitment either. The Lord was about to reject them as one of His. He says in verse 16,

> *"So because you are lukewarm—neither hot nor cold—I am about to spit you out of my mouth."*

Other translations use the word "spew" or "vomit" out of His mouth. This would lead us to believe that God is intensely serious when our commitment to Him is middle of the road.

Back in this day, when letters came, they were read aloud to the church. I'm sure the comparison of them to the lukewarm water that Jesus wanted to spit out, got their attention. They had grown complacent and unwilling to take a stand for God and His Word.

Complacent Christians are those who receive Jesus, but live as though He makes no difference in their daily lives. He refers to three key things from verse 17:

1. Jesus refers to their wealth and speaks of their attitude of- *"I am rich; I have acquired wealth and do not need a thing"* (3:17). The church supposed it had such adequate material resources that it could do without the Lord's spiritual help.
2. He calls them *"naked"* at the end of verse 17. He makes mention of clothes and coverings in verse 18, referencing the textile industry that was prominent there. The church's attitude could suggest that they thought they were clothed with plenty of righteous character.
3. Jesus also calls them *"blind."* I guess they thought they had spiritual insight on matters. The "blind" comment is referring to their famous eye salve to help people see. But they were also blind to Gods ways.

What's saddest and most frightening is that in verse 17 Jesus says they do not even realize their condition. Are we complacent like this too? Do we only seek the Lord when we need Him? Like the loving Father that He is, He says to us,

> *"Those whom I love I rebuke and discipline. Here I am. I stand at the door and knock. If anyone hears my voice and opens the door, I will come in and eat with him and he with Me."*
>
> Revelation 3:20

He's never far. He's always right by our side. We are the ones who push Him back, close the door or turn away.

Warner Sallman was a gifted American artist and illustrator born in 1892. During the war years of the 1940's, his popular and sympathetic *Head of Christ* inspired and comforted millions of people. You've probably seen it, even if you don't recognize the name. Sallman created another, perhaps equally as famous representation of Jesus called *Christ at the Door,* drawn from Revelation 3:20. (You can see either of these wonderful painting by doing a simple online search of Sallman's name.)

The Christ figure is standing patiently, just about to knock. The archways of the door and the porch roof are from a perfect heart shape, emphasized by the lighting. The door itself - unlike any real door - has no outside latch.[7]

Obviously, Sallman understood Revelation 3:20 to be speaking of Jesus' knocking at the door of an individual's life. But as we have learned, Christ shouldn't be waiting to knock and ask to come in. He should be inside. Are we living with Him in mind?

The book of Revelation was sent to real churches with real spiritual problems. Jesus challenged them to be overcomers, but He never expected them, or us, to do it alone. He puts Himself in the midst of the churches, walking among them in fellowship.

Is He walking with you? Or have you let something come between you that is straining your fellowship with Him? Go to Him. Let Him in your heart. He will transform your life.

Endnotes:

1. Community Bible Study TD Helps; 2008; Lesson 4; pg 11
2. Kendall Easely, Revelation- Holman New Testament Commentary 1998 B & H Publishing Group; Nashville,TN; pg 64
3. Ibid., pg 54
4. Ibid., pg 64, 65
5. Ibid., pg 56
6. Ibid., pg 66, 67
7. Kendall Easely, Revelation- Holman New Testament Commentary 1998 B & H Publishing Group; Nashville,TN; pg 53

CHAPTER 4

"Then the King [Solomon] made a great throne inlaid with ivory and overlaid with find gold. The throne had six steps, and its back had a rounded top. On both sides of the seat were armrests, with a lion standing beside each of them. Twelve lions stood on the six steps, one at either end of each step. Nothing like it had ever been made for any other kingdom."

1 Kings 10:18-20

As magnificent as Solomon's great throne sounds in this description, it is still man-made. God shows us His throne room in this chapter and it is…well…heavenly.

Have you ever seen a lightning storm in the evening hours? They're glorious! Night falls, clouds build way up high, rumbling with thunder and lightning. There is so much activity from the flashing inside the clouds. I can't help but think about the throne room of God and how powerful and awe-inspiring that must be. How electrifying the atmosphere must be, all because of worship to our God and Father.

I will never look at lightning storms the same again after having read this chapter. I come back to this imagery and think of His magnificence every time I hear thunder and see lighting. It's just all so glorious!

As chapter 4 opens, Christ summons John to come through a heavenly door to see what normally is closed off to human vision. But this is not the first time heaven's doors have been opened for such a glimpse. Let's look at some other examples.

The prophet Ezekiel had a vision of heaven:

"In the thirtieth year, in the fourth month on the fifth day, while I

*was among the exiles by the Kebar River, the heavens were opened
and I saw visions of God."*

Ezekiel 1:1

In the New Testament, God again showed us heaven's door:

*"As soon as Jesus was baptized, He went up out of the water. At
that moment heaven was opened, and He saw the Spirit of God
descending like a dove and alighting Him."*

Matthew 3:16

Again, right before Stephen is dragged out and stoned to death:

*"Look", he said, "I see heaven open and the son of Man standing
at the right hand of God."*

Acts 7:56

And once more, when Peter saw a vision of "unclean" animals:

*"He saw heaven opened and something like a large sheet being let
down to earth by its four corners."*

Acts 10:11

These are just glimpses, but now John (and we along with him as we
read) is taken even deeper into heaven. We are privileged to enter where
no living human is typically invited. Jesus tells John to write down
everything he sees. Clearly God *wants* us to see Him in His entire
splendor. (We'll look into heaven three more times as we continue to
study Revelation.) 4:1 tells of His voice again as a trumpet sound. In
chapter 1:11, Christ's first command to John had been: *"Write on a scroll
what you see."* Here in 4:1, the command is *"Come up here and I will show you
what must take place after this."* Jesus is the true revealer. This is a reminder
that the contents of Revelation belong to Jesus. All the events must take
place, whether we think of the terrible events or the blessed ones. The
"must" is emphatic. The future is determined and God is in control of
it all. There is comfort in remembering that. This point was to encourage
the seven churches as well as discipline them.

Do you remember NASA's Apollo 13 space flight from 1970? If that
true event was before your time, perhaps you watched the Oscar Award-
winning movie that was based on the event. Three astronauts on their
way to the moon experience a crippling explosion that damages their
rocketship. Lovett, Swaggart and Hayes, alone in space, struggle to stay
alive and return to earth. *Houston, we have a problem.* At mission control,

director Gene Kranz and all the men under his command work diligantly to put a plan together to get the astronauts back home. They concentrate on every minute detail, because every minute detail was critical. The director was not about to lose those men on his watch. The mission was carried out with perfection and the astronauts returned home safely.[1]

We all may have different ideas about the church, the Great Tribulation, and where the rapture fits in (pre-, mid-, or post-tribulation). We don't really know for sure; we can only speculate. Scripture is unclear, and we may disagree on our interpretation of it. But we can agree on one thing that is clear: This is God's mission, and He is in control.

He has made a covenant with His church, and told them that all who call on His name and believe in Him will be saved, and that one day He will see us return home safely.

That is God's mission. If you fear the future, remember God is in control. He has a plan and His plan is just, because He is sovereign. He has His eye on every minute detail.

Even as John is writing down what he is seeing, he has to grasp for words to describe the splendor and majesty of what he sees. He uses comparisons and similes. The One who sat on the throne had the *appearance* of jasper and carnelian (4:3), there was a rainbow *resembling* an emerald (4:3), *it was like* a sea of glass, clear as crystal (4:6). And there, in the middle of it all, on the throne seat is the power of the universe, the maker of Heaven and Earth, the beginning and the end, God Almighty - the Great I AM.

> *"Surrounding the throne were twenty-four other thrones, and seated on them were twenty-four elders. They were dressed in white and had crowns of gold on their heads."*

Revelation 4:4

The clothing indicates a close association with heavenly beings, because angels, as well as saints, are said to wear white. Matthew 28:3 describes Jesus in appearance after He was resurrected from the dead;

> *"His appearance was like lightning, and his clothes were white as snow."*

The crowns represented authority, just like an earthy crown would. Some commentaries have suggested that these elders represent either the 12 tribes of Israel from the Old Testament and the 12 apostles of the New Testament, and/or some kind of heavenly ruling council.[2]

The number 24 seems to indicate a group of representatives, just like the divisions of the priests that were mentioned in 1 Chronicles 24:1-19. They were divided into 24 groups, each with a chief over it. These elders are closely associated with two other kinds of heavenly beings: the angels and the four living creatures.[3]

In verses 6-8 the four living creatures are described as having eyes covering the front and back. These creatures were *like* a lion, an ox, a man and a flying eagle who all had six wings each. In Ezekiel's vision of heaven he describes these creatures in a similar manner, but adds this:

> *"The creatures sped back and forth like flashes of lightning."*
>
> Ezekiel 1:14

This suggests they all move about rapidly and are constantly evaluating the environment of God's throne to assure holiness.

Some commentators say the four creatures represent attributes of God's character. For example, the all-seeing eyes covering each creature picture God's omnipresence and His omniscience. He sees and knows everything. The lion as king of beasts represents his royalty. The ox illustrates His ability to carry our burdens. The eagle can soar to great heights, pointing us to His sovereignty. Finally, the man's face symbolizes God's crowning work in creation: mankind - you and me. When John looks at the creatures worshipping God, he understands more of what God is like.[4] It's a beautiful picture.

> *"Holy, holy, holy the LORD God Almighty, who was and is and is to come."*
>
> Revelation 4:8

The 24 elders fall down before God. This shows that whatever authority and rank they may have, ultimately comes from Him, because it is He who awarded them their crowns. They will know that their privilege is because of His grace and for that, He is due all praise. In return, the elders' praise recognizes that God created all things. Only by His will did anything come into being. As John was witnessing this vision of glory, I wonder if he was remembering what he wrote in his gospel years earlier.

> *"Through Him all things were made; without Him nothing was made that has been made."*
>
> John 1:3

During John's time, for the believers under persecution from Rome, this mention of the holiness of the true God was comforting. The world was becoming decadent, and evil seemed to be prevailing.

Thrones always symbolize the power and rule of the sovereign who sits there. Here, the Throne of God actually appears before John. This throne is over all other thrones. In contrast, the throne of Rome was ruled by an evil and godless pagan who claimed to be a god - Domitian. Only the true throne room, and the Holy God who sits on it, is ruled by sovereignty, in holiness and righteousness.

We are all getting tired of the world's decadence, and yet, sometimes we're the cause of it. The world today and its challenges seem to be similar to the world then. Isn't it comforting to think that one day God will rid the world of sin, evil, decay and filth and even purify it? I love that thought.

Holiness is God's essential character. Shouldn't we, therefore, strive to live a holy life? God is the only One who is holy, but we should make it our goal to live a complete and pure life. This honors God and brings Him glory, but He knows we can't do that on our own. He loves us enough to provide what we cannot produce. That's why He gave us a Savior. We should thank Him for that, and thank Him often. He has washed us clean and made us holy by His blood.

God is Sovereign. God is holy. He is worthy of all praise. He is God our Father. He is the maker of heaven and of earth. Only God is worthy of honor, worship and praise!

Corrie Ten Boom was one of God's twentieth century saints. Imprisoned by the Nazi's for hiding Jews in her home during World War II, she survived years of horrible circumstances in the concentration camp she was sent to, and after her release she began to testify around the world about God's grace in the worst of situations. Whenever anyone praised her, she would refuse to take that credit for herself and immediately laid that praise at God's feet. What a great example for us to follow.[5]

There is much discussion in churches about whether a worship style should be traditional or contemporary. The elders in the throne room teach us that true worship cannot be orchestrated. Style is not the issue. Worship is a spontaneous movement of the heart, and God is always about the heart. True worship comes from having the right heart posture as you look into the face of the living God.

If you have been blessed with "crowns" in this life (achievements, rewards, praises, etc.) remember the Source of your blessing. Cast your crowns at His feet, for He alone is worthy of glory and praise. Crowns can also be the opportunities for having done good things too. These are the types of things that no one may see on the outside, but only God will see (or know about). Thank Him for the opportunity that you were given, and praise Him for that!

A children's book by Robert E. Wells asks; "Is the Blue Whale the Biggest Thing There Is?"

> *"The blue whale is the largest animal on earth. Its flippers alone are bigger than most animals. BUT the blue whale is small compared to a mountain. You could put millions of blue whales in a hollowed out Mt. Everest. And Mt. Everest is small compared to the earth. One hundred Mt. Everest's stacked on top of one another would just be a whisker on the face of the earth. One million earth's would fit into the sun. And the sun is just a medium-sized star. Fifty million suns could fit in a red super giant star named Antares. But Antares is small compared to the Milky Way galaxy. Billions of stars like Anatares make up the Milky Way. And billions of galaxies make up the universe."[6]*

The Creator of it all is the LORD God Almighty. With a word, He spoke it all into being. He is present everywhere in this universe and beyond, holding all things together with His mighty power, yet He is so intimate with each of us. He knew us in our mothers' wombs (Jeremiah 1:5) and even knows how many hairs are on our heads. (Luke 12:7).

God is in control of it all - yes, even satan himself - and God has a plan for the end of this world. Need a little more convincing? A very wise, respected lecturer and Bible teacher named Phyllis Cooper said it best: when we think about what God wants us to know with the revealing of this book, He's in all the details.

> *"The use of numbers in Revelation is a fascinating study. Even when they can be interpreted literally, they often have a symbolic meaning as well. The number "7" appears fifty-four times in Revelation, more than any other number. The Hebrews considered it a sacred number because it was the number of the Sabbath, making it stand for completion of perfection. Use of this number*

may indicate a complete group of something. We have already seen the 7 churches that represent a complete picture of the problems of any church. Then there are the 7 lampstands, the 7 stars, and the 7 spirits of God. Yet to come are the 7 plagues, 7 thunders, 7 thousand killed, a 7-headed dragon with 7 crowns, a 7-headed beast, 7 mountains, and 7 kings. God's order is perfect and complete. The Sovereign Lord is orchestrating every bit of the future. Nothing "just happens."

God is in control of it all. Period. There is no need to fear.

Endnotes:

1. Community Bible Study TD Helps; 2008; Lesson 5; pg 13
2. NIV Study Bible 1985 by the Zondervan Corperation, commentary notes, pg 1931
3. Community Bible Study Revelation Commentary by Timothy Carter, 1997,2004 ; Lesson 5, pg.3
4. Community Bible Study Revelation "Think about"; by Phyllis Cooper, 1997-2004; Lesson 5, pg 6
5. Community Bible Study TD Helps; 2008; Lesson 5; pg 15
6. Is the Blue Whale the Biggest Thing There Is? 1998, by Robert E.Wells; Published by Whittman and Co.
7. Community Bible Study Revelation "Think about"; by Phyllis Cooper, 1997-2004; Lesson 5, pg 4

Chapter 5

"You awaken us to delight in your praise; for you have made us for yourself, and our hearts are restless until they rest in you."

St. Augustine

Having already described the incredible heavenly setting and what he saw, John now experiences a profound event that has eternal importance, and all of this takes place before God's throne. This chapter reveals the initiation of the astonishing events that will ultimately culminate in the final end of the kingdoms of this age.

John sees God Himself seated on the throne and notices in His right hand a scroll, or book. John notes that it has writing on not just one side, but both sides. Normally a scroll is only written on the inside, so this indicates that this scroll contains many details.

God has communicated through His writings to us like this before - originally on tablets made of stone. They were the called...*a-hem*...the Ten Commandments.

"Moses turned and went down the mountain with the two tablets of the Testimony in his hands. They were inscribed on both sides, front and back."

Exodus 32:15

After the prophet Ezekiel's visions of God's throne, His glory there, and the four living creatures (Ezekiel 1:4-28), he also saw the hand of God outstretched.

"Then I looked and I saw a hand stretched out to me. In it was a scroll, which he unrolled before me. On both sides of it were written words of lament and mourning and woe."

Ezekiel 2:9-10

(God has been taking notes on us.)

Zechariah warns the people of Israel from his vision of writings on both sides of a *flying* scroll.

> *"This is the curse that is going out over the whole land; for according to what it says on one side, every thief will be banished, and according to what it says on the other, everyone who swears falsely will be banished."*
>
> Zechariah 5:3

This scroll described in chapter 5 could be the same scroll described in the Ezekiel and Zechariah passages. This seems to be God's Judgment Scroll.

Some say it is the deed the Father gave to His Son, the Lamb who was slain, giving Him authority to rule in the coming kingdom. Others say it contains the prophetic record of God's judgment and fulfillment of His plan to redeem those Jesus purchased by His blood. Some say it contains both - God's purpose for history and the deed of authority.[1]

In either case, it holds the mystery of God's final plan for the world.

But now it is sealed with not one seal, but seven seals. This is the complete plan of God.

Daniel 12:9 says they must remain *"closed up and sealed until the time of the end"* – the very period addressed here in Revelation. Then a mighty angel proclaims in a loud voice: *"Who is worthy to break the seals and open the scroll?"* God is the One who made the plan and authorized the scroll to be closed, so God's Son is the only One who is worthy to enact the plan by opening the scroll.[2]

There were many angels that surrounded the throne, so why couldn't one of them open the scroll? Aren't these heavenly beings sinless? That's not the point. Only a sinless man, a perfect man, could redeem the world that Adam lost dominion over when he sinned. Realizing this, John weeps for mankind's failure, and he weeps for his own.[3]

W. A. Criswell, in his *Expository Sermons on Revelation* describes man's condition through the apostle Johns tears:

> *"John's tears represent the tears of all God's people through all the centuries. They're the tears of Adam and Eve as they view the still form of their dead son, Abel, and sense the awful consequences of their disobedience. They are the tears of the children of Israel in*

bondage as they cried to God for deliverance from their affliction and slavery. They're the sobs of God's people as they have stood beside the graves of loved ones and experienced the indescribable heartaches and disappointments of life.

"Such is the curse that sin has laid upon God's beautiful creation. No wonder John wept so fervently. If no redeemer could be found to remove the curse, it meant that God's creation was forever consigned to remain in the hand of satan."[4]

In 5:5 one of these 24 elders comes to John with good news. He says, *"do not weep."* There is someone who is qualified to break open the sealed up scroll. Then John hears unique titles for this worthy One in verses 5:5-6, and each title refers to the Messiah:

- **The Lion of the Tribe of Judah** - The prophecy regarding the royal line came through Jacob's blessing on his son Judah (Genesis 49:8-10). Jacob had 12 sons, one of the sons' tribes, Judah, would rule over all the other tribes. King David came from this tribe as did all the other rulers that succeeded him. Jesus is called the "Son of David" in the gospels and Judah's line would provide kings for the entire nation of Israel, ultimately fulfilled by the Messiah. The Lion of Judah symbolizes monarchy or royalty.

- **The Root of David** - When King David's line was cut off from reigning in Israel during the time of the Babylonian captivity, the root still remained, meaning the line was still there. Christ is the only One alive who can trace His line back to David, and before to Judah. The One from the Root of David is clearly the Messiah, Jesus, for He is the rightful descendant of David.

- **A Lamb, looking as if it had been slain** - This is no ordinary lamb. This Lamb bears the scars of death. Those scars remind us of the tremendous love of Jesus Christ, poured out for us at the cross.[5] Remember Isaiah 53:5? It says, *"But he was pierced for our transgressions, he was crushed for our iniquities; the punishment that brought us peace was on him, and by his wounds we are healed."*

I want to remind us of the number seven again and its significance as it pertains to the Lambs description. The Lamb has seven horns and seven eyes. The number seven denotes His omnipotence. The seven eyes signify the all-seeing, omniscient Holy Spirit.

Then in verse 5:7, He came and took the scroll from the right hand of God, thereby claiming ownership of it. The Son perfectly carries out what the Father has determined. Remember, Rev. 1: 1 says, *"The revelation of Jesus Christ which God gave Him."* God wants us to know Christ as the ultimate authority.

In her book, *Vision of Glory,* Ann Graham Lotz gives a perspective that is worth pondering.

> *"If He is undisputed in His power in the universe—and He is— why do we argue with Him, resisting His claim on our lives? He created you and me. He bought us at Calvary, and He is the ONLY One who has the right to rule our lives."*

She goes on to say:

> *"You and I need to stop resisting His will, stop arguing about His purpose, stop complaining about His methods, and just submit to His authority. How ashamed we will be one day to discover that we were the only ones in the entire universe disputing the authority of the Lamb. We need to change our arrogant attitude and fall in step with the rest of the universe that does not resist, but praises Him."*[6]

Once Jesus (the Lamb) takes the scroll from God (without objection and without delay, I may add), the immediate response of the 24 elders was to worship the Lamb (Christ), and the four living creatures join in, falling down and worshipping (5:7-8). He has redeemed us. It was the "once and for all" work that Jesus did on the cross that finds Him alone worthy.

> *"Therefore God exalted Him to the highest place and gave Him the name that is above every name, that at the name of Jesus every knee should bow in heaven and on earth and under the earth, and every tongue confess that Jesus Christ is Lord, to the glory of God the Father."*
>
> Philippians 2:9-11

The rest of verse eight says, each one of the heavenly beings *"had a harp, and they were holding golden bowls of incense - which are the prayers of the saints."* The golden bowls of incense were shallow, saucer-like. They would fill the air with a fragrant smoke.

This was what Aaron was instructed to do when in the tabernacle. Every morning when Aaron maintains the lamps, he must burn fragrant incense on the altar (Exodus 30:7, NLT)

David compared his prayers, rising to God, to the smoke of incense in Psalm 141:2:

> "May my prayer be set before You like incense; may this lifting up of my hands be like the evening sacrifice."

We'll see the same symbolism in chapter 8. The point is, be encouraged when you pray. When the saints on earth praise and pray to Christ, their worship is received by Christ in heaven. Scripture constantly teaches that the prayers of God's people impact the throne of heaven. But here in these verses, is a vivid, visual representation of this truth. Be encouraged. Your prayers are being heard.[7]

They sing a new song in 5:10.

> "Every tribe, language, people, and nation will be made into a kingdom of priests to serve God and they will reign on earth."

This is referring to Israel in the Old Testament, and in the New Testament this applies to the church universal - the body of Christ.

The prophet Zechariah gives a prophecy about the defeat of Israel's enemies and the Messiah's return.

> "On that day his feet will stand on the Mount of Olives, east of Jerusalem, and the Mount of Olives will be split in two from east to west, forming a great valley, with half of the mountain moving north and half moving south. You will flee by my mountain valley, for it will extend to Azel. You will flee as you fled from the earthquake in the days of Uzziah, king of Judah. Then the Lord my God will come, and all the holy ones with Him. On that day there will be neither sunlight nor cold, frosty darkness. It will be a unique day—a day known only to the Lord—with no distinction between day and night. When evening comes, there will be light. On that day living water will flow out from Jerusalem, half of it east to the Dead Sea and half of it west to the Mediterranean Sea, in summer and in winter. The Lord will be king over the whole earth. On that day there will be one Lord, and His name the only name."
>
> Zechariah 14:4-9

This just gets me excited. *This* is Who we worship.

Verses 11-12 say,

> *"Then I looked and heard the voice of many angels, numbering thousands upon thousands, and ten thousand times ten thousand."*

That's more than 100 million of the hosts of heaven!

Here's a fun fact:

The number for 10,000 was the largest that the Greek language could express, so this is an *incalculable* multitude.[8]

"Worthy is the Lamb that was slain," is what they sing in 5:12.

Think of a football stadium or an Olympic stadium full of angels with them all praising God's Holy name. Now multiply it by the biggest number you know. Just picture that sight. Wow! The next time you go to a game in a stadium, take a moment to look around you and think about the heavenly throne room of God and all the praises there. It's simply magnificent to ponder!

Jesus first came to us as a lowly child, confined in a human body. Now He is in the highest place that God has to give. All throughout Revelation Christ is described (when talking about the throne room of God) as the Lamb. He could have been referred to as the Lion of Judah, but instead He is described as the Lamb, our redeemer. The One who overcame death and sin for us. Our problems don't seem so overwhelming when we compare them to the Lamb of God, our Redeemer, do they? He is able. This is the majestic picture of heaven. We should live as if earth were heaven. Why do I say that? Colossians 3:1-2 says:

> *"Since then, you have been raised with Christ, set you hearts on things above where Christ is seated at the right hand of God. Set your mind on things above not on earthly things."*

The Lord's Prayer says:

> *"Thy Kingdom come, Thy will be done on earth, as it is in heaven."*

The two are connected more than we realize. If we can set (or train) our hearts and our minds on things above (which means heaven), and really live this way, it will truly be heaven on earth for us.

That is living a victorious life!

One day we will praise Him with the rest of the universe - whether we want to or not. The Apostle Paul reminds us what Christ said in Romans 4:11:

> *"'As surely as I live,' says the Lord, 'every knee will bow before me; every tongue will acknowledge God.'"*

And in Philippians 2:10, "Every" means *every*.

> *"...that at the name of Jesus every knee should bow, in heaven and on earth and under the earth."*

Why don't we start now? Isn't He alone worthy of our praise, our heart, our destiny, our trust and our devotion?

I'll end this chapter with this point:

Perhaps we have praised God as our Creator, but have we bowed down before Jesus Christ, our Redeemer?

Trust Him. He is worthy.

Endnotes:

1. Community Bible Study TD Helps; 2008; Lesson 6; pg 16
2. Kendall Easely, Revelation- Holman New Testament Commentary 1998 B & H Publishing Group; Nashville,TN; pg 91
3. Community Bible Study Revelation "Think about"; by Phyllis Cooper, 1997-2004; Lesson 6, pg 2
4. 2012 The W. A. Criswell Foundation. All Rights Reserved.
5. Community Bible Study TD Helps; 2008; Lesson 6; pg 17
6. Vision Of Glory by Ann Graham Lotz, published by Word Publishing (June 4, 1997)
7. Kendall Easely, Revelation- Holman New Testament Commentary 1998 B & H Publishing Group; Nashville,TN; pg 94
8. Ibid., pg 95

CHAPTER 6

The definition of Tribulation is: "a state or cause of great trouble and suffering."

The noun - tribulation ("thlipsis" Greek) is found 43 times in the New Testament. Its basic idea is to apply pressure in a negative situation. Our English word comes from the Latin "tribulum," the harrow or threshing instrument used to separate grain from its husk.

Let me explain the threshing experience first, so you can better understand the point being made.

There are dozens of references to a "threshing floor" in the Bible, some literal and some symbolic. In biblical days there was no automated method of threshing grain. After the harvest, the grain was separated from the straw and husks by beating it manually. First there had to be a flat surface that was smooth and hard. This was known as the threshing floor. The process of threshing was performed by spreading the sheaves on the threshing floor, then causing oxen and cattle to tread repeatedly over them, loosening the edible part of cereal grain (or other crop) from the scaly, inedible chaff that surrounds it. On occasion, flails or sticks were used for this purpose. Once the chaff had been separated from the grain, winnowing forks were used to throw the mixture into the air so the wind could blow away the chaff, leaving only the good grain on the floor.[1]

The definition of "threshing" means literally, "to trample out."[2]

There once was a man who fretted about how the Great Tribulation might affect him. He became convinced that he needed to stock pile food for his family. He didn't want anyone to starve during the severe famine or in case Christians were forbidden to purchase anything during the coming days of the crisis. He invested a substantial amount of savings into hundreds of cans of specially processed food, everything from whole-wheat flour to peanut butter to dried banana flakes. He gathered enough to feed his family (sparingly) for three years. All the goods had a guaranteed shelf life of at least 10 years. He died four years later, leaving row upon row of cans untouched. Finally, 15 years later, his family disposed of all of it. It was a total loss.

We all experience some type of tribulation, and yes, scripture tells us of a Great Tribulation to come - but you cannot physically prepare for it. The only way through it is to prepare for it spiritually.

During these next few chapters, I want us to rely on the fact that Christ is on the throne and He is in control. We have to aline ourselves with Him and Him alone, otherwise we will be trampled out. He is the only way through these times, if we are alive when it comes. Always keep in mind as we walk through these coming chapters what Jesus tells us at the end of John 10:10; *"...take heart, I have overcome the world."*

Chapter 6 opens with Jesus, the Lamb, breaking the first seal and that sets forth the horsemen and the judgments. This is the beginning of The Tribulation period. However, these events only set the stage for the contents of the scroll itself.

Perspective is everything as we study this book. Yes, there will be tribulation and even if we're the ones who live during it, our perspective is we're Christ's and this is not our home. Take heart, Christ has overcome the world.

Listen to what Jesus warns His followers about.

> *"Watch out that no one deceives you. Many will come in My name, claiming, 'I am he', and will deceive many. When you hear of wars and rumors of wars, do not be alarmed. Such things must happen, but the end is still to come. Nation will rise against nation and kingdom against kingdom. There will be earthquakes in various places, and famines. These are the beginning of birth pains... Brother will betray brother to death and a father his child. Children will rebel against their parents and have them put to death. All men will hate you because of Me, but he who stands firm to the end will be saved."*

Mark 13:12-13

The overlap about what Jesus foretold and what John reported when the Lamb broke the seals is startling. John, who was present for both events, understood Jesus is the same man who prophesied this and so the circumstances to come will happen. It's the same language.

Jesus (the Lamb), already knew when He spoke this, what to expect from the breaking of each seal on the scroll.

Here's something else to think about; all seven seals must be removed in order for God's Judgment Scroll of the future to be opened. This means that we should not expect any special or final end-time events to be revealed until after all seven seals are broken (And that begins in a later chapter).

The Horsemen

Ok, let's begin to review the horsemen. Verse two talks about the first horseman. But God gave us a hint of this back in the Old Testament. God revealed a vision to Zechariah even then.

In Zechariah 1:10, Zechariah sees in his vision four men with four horses and an angel tells him, *"They are the ones the LORD has sent to go throughout the earth."* Then in Zechariah 6:5 he sees four chariots with red, black, white and dappled (spotted) horses, which are *"...the four spirits of heaven, going out from standing in the presence of the Lord of the whole world."* The horses are harnessed to the chariots.

God reveals His plan many times to us. Why? He wants us to be prepared and He wants no one to perish. You will begin to see God's compassion in this book and His heart as well. We are *His* creation and *His* children. God measures out His judgment in an ever-intensifying succession. As we read the power given to each of the four horsemen, the truth begins to dawn on us - God is simply allowing man to self-destruct. Man's ambition to conquer drives him to bloody wars. Wars lead to economic crisis and that leads to famine. Famines lead to plagues, disease and death. Those who stand for Jesus are murdered. Yet, in the perfect time - God intervenes.

The Breaking Open of the First Seal - A White Horse and Its Rider:

John sees a white horse in 6:2. But the rider rather than the horse interested John. The White horseman *"came out conquering, and to conquer."* This speaks of a conqueror bent on conquest, which is probably of a military type – an aggressor that is being set loose.

Commentator Timothy Crater explains it this way:

> *"Who is this rider? Scholars suggest totally opposing views. Some point to the white horse and say that its rider must be Christ (referring to Rev. 19:11). Others say that he must be the antichrist, pointing out that Christ will come after the Tribulation, not before. However, given that he is the first of four riders/ horses with strong Old Testaments mentions, it is possible that the first horse and rider represent a spirit- ("the four spirits of heaven" Zechariah 6:5) of conquest, of martial aggression that is being set loose on the earth by God's seal decree."*[8]

Next to him is a bow. This would suggest some kind of war. But notice there is *no arrow* mentioned. Remember the Cold War? Wars nowadays can be fought in cyberspace. Leaders will seek world domination by political power. It is possible it will be domination of economic power due to the famine that will take place. The giving of a crown would suggest some type of political power. The crown is not a "royal" crown. The Greek word ("stephanos") refers to a winner's crown, like a laurel. This rider could reflect man's sinful heart as stated in James 4:1-2:

> *"What causes fights and quarrels among you? Don't they come from your desires that battle within you? You want something but don't get it. You kill and covet, but you cannot have what you want. You quarrel and fight."*

God also used a spirit like this to entice King Ahab. In 2 Chronicles 18, the kingdoms of Israel were still divided. King Ahab (King of Israel), wants to go to war against the king of Aram at Ramoth Gilead and he wants King Jehoshaphat (King of Judah) to join him. Ahab is not a good man. In fact, he is a greedy and wicked king. Micaiah, son of Imiah, is a prophet of the Lord who Ahab does not like because he always seems to prophecy against the king. But Ahab is forced to ask for him to speak his prophecy because Jehoshaphat requests it, and again, this prophecy is not favorable towards Ahab. Here is what Micaiah prophesied:

> *"Therefore hear the word of the Lord: I saw the Lord sitting on his throne with all the multitudes of heaven standing on his right and on his left. And the Lord said, 'Who will entice Ahab king of Israel into attacking Ramoth Gilead and going to his death there?' One suggested this, and another that. Finally, a spirit came forward, stood before the Lord and said, 'I will entice him.'*

'By what means?' the Lord asked.
'I will go and be a deceiving spirit in the mouths of all his prophets,'
he said. 'You will succeed in enticing him,' said the Lord. 'Go and
do it.'"

2 Chronicles 18:18-21

Everything around us is spiritual. This spirit of the White horseman is bent on conquest. If you couple that with what James said about man's desire for battle, you begin to get a realization of what man will be like when this spirit is unleashed - wicked and greedy, just like Ahab. Maybe humankind is that way already? Either way, God is in control of the unfolding of it all. That is the point I wanted to make here. Nothing takes God by surprise. This has all been carefully crafted and planned out.

The Breaking Open of the Second Seal - A Red Horse and Its Rider:

The White horseman suggests conqueror and conquest, and even though this spirit does not use his arrow, this doesn't mean that after the conquest that there won't be a war. The Red horseman is not just described as "red," but "fiery red." This might suggest bloody warfare to come. Scripture explicitly states in 6:4, that this rider *"was given power to take peace from the earth and to make men slay each other."* So there will be bloodshed. He was also given a large sword to fight with. Not a dagger or a sharp knife - but a large sword. This would imply a bloody warfare to come.

When you combine the greedy conquering attitude that is set forth from the White horseman, this tells me wickedness will be everywhere prior to the bloodshed that the Red horseman will bring. I believe God lets sinful man turn on himself.

That's what I feel will happen here. But also remember, God is in control of all of this too. Now I know I sound like a broken record, but we can easily focus on the horror of all of this and forget that He's the one orchestrating this. He wants us to be aware and be prepared so we will have wisdom and discernment to hear Him and He will guide us through all of this. In Isaiah 19:2 we're reminded:

"There is no peace for the wicked."

This will be a time of great chaos. Paul says in 1 Thessalonians 5:3-4:

"While people are saying, "Peace and safety," destruction will come on them suddenly, as labor pains on a pregnant woman, and they will not escape. But you, brothers and sisters, are not in darkness so that this day should surprise you like a thief."

Right here in this scripture, God is letting us know that He wants us to be informed and prepared. During this time the peace that the wicked will long for, (apart from God), will elude them. The rider on the Red horse will be the one to take it away.

The Breaking Open of the Third Seal; A Black Horse and Its Rider:

The Black horseman suggests food scarcity and famine. When there's war, famine is usually a natural result. The color of the horse is significant because in the Old Testament, black is associated with the effects of famine and starvation. Job says this about himself:

"My skin grows black and peels; my body burns with fever."

Job 30:30

The author of Lamentations laments on what life was like after the destruction of Jerusalem:

"But now they are blacker than soot; they are not recognized in the streets. Their skin has shriveled on their bones; it has become as dry as a stick."

Lamentations 4:8

The scales that the rider carries in 6:5 are important to note as well. When food is precious it is weighed out carefully. In Ezekiel 4:16, God says to Jerusalem's inhabitants:

"The people will eat rationed food in anxiety and drink rationed water in despair."

Also in Leviticus 26:26 God tells the Israelites how bad things will be if they are disobedient.

"When I cut off your supply of bread, ten women will be able to bake your bread in one oven, and they will dole out the bread by weight. You will eat, but you will not be satisfied."

Timothy Crater's commentary again, gives us a clearer picture:

> *"From the midst of the four creatures, a voice decrees the measure of scarcity for food. The average daily pay of a working man, a denarius, would normally buy eight quarts of wheat or twenty-four quarts of the cheaper barley, the poor man's grain. The amount of wheat cited here, "a quart," was the average daily ration for one man. Grain would become so scarce that it would take a man's whole daily wage just to buy his own daily grain ration, with little left for his family or other needs. The frustration of hunger as well as the economic crisis because of the shortage of food will contribute further to the violent, hostile climate engendered by the first two riders."[5]*

Notice also that the horseman is not allowed to damage the oil and the wine. We have to remember, God is orchestrating all of this and *they are limited* by what God says to do and not to do.

The Breaking Open of the Fourth Seal; A Pale Horse and Its Rider:

This horse is pale or ashen, depicting death - which is a fitting hue for him. This horseman has an assistant - a brother-type character that verse 6:8 says follows close behind. His name is Hades. Picture him on foot or mounted behind the rider, Death. Either way they go hand in hand. Hades (the grave, the place of the dead), is to pick up after Death does his work. God gives them the power to take out one fourth (a quarter) of the world at this time.

Again, let me point out that things like calamity and evil must have God's authorization. The deadly twosome may destroy four distinct ways: by sword, by famine, by plague or by wild beasts. These four forms of death were familiar to the prophets in the Old Testament. In Ezekiel 14:21 God calls them His "four dreadful judgments."

> *"For this is what the Sovereign Lord says: How much worse will it be when I send against Jerusalem my four dreadful judgments - sword and famine and wild beasts and plague - to kill its men and their animals."*

Hades is mentioned in Revelation four times, and it is always trailing death. As horrible as they are, their power is limited. It's what Christ permits, and He has given them the authority for this time.

The tribulation is a time of great distress, yes, but do not be deceived.

God has offered a plan to save us and that is through Jesus Christ, our Lord and Savior. But you may ask, "What about family members and/or friends who do not know Jesus?" Now is the time, while we are able to do all we can to get people into the Word of God and understanding who God really is and what His character is all about.

Knowledge is power, and understanding our Creator is key. Let's start with our communities. Let's bring them to church or attend a Bible study together. Learn about the power of prayer and the importance it has in covering our nation and its leaders. Know God, and know how important *prayers* are to God. Prayer can change circumstances and lives. Invest in that knowledge. Let's keep praying, and trusting that our prayers are reaching our King. There's power in this act of obedience. Prayer can change lives. Prayer can *save* lives!

The Breaking Open of the Fifth Seal; Souls Under the Altar:

This prophecy moves us from earthly judgments to the heavenly saints. Under this heavenly altar, John sees and identifies *"the souls that had been slain"* for Christ (6:9).

Hebrews 8:5 mentions that the earthly tabernacle in the Old Testament was a copy or shadow of the heavenly one - the true throne room with the altar of God present.[7] The souls are here, sheltered in a sacred and holy place close to God. These believers had been martyred for the Word of God and for their testimony. They had faithfully held fast to the testimony about Christ, and their witness cost them their lives on earth.

They plead with God to avenge them and ask, *"How long Oh God?"* His answer for now is found in verse 11. God consoles them by giving them a white robe, and tells them to wait a little while longer. The white robe reflects righteousness in God's sight. Remember what Jesus said to the church of Sardis?

> *"Yet you have a few people in Sardis who have not soiled their clothes. They will walk with Me, dressed in white, for they are worthy."*

> Revelation 3:4

God will avenge them on His time table. He does not work within our understanding of time. According to the rest of verse 11, there is a plan that needs to be complete before God will avenge, and His timing will be perfect.

We must not avenge ourselves, even if we are able. We need to leave that to God. Jesus says so in Romans 12:19-21:

> *"Do not take revenge, my dear friends, but leave room for God's wrath, for it is written: 'It is mine to avenge; I will repay,' says the Lord. On the contrary: If your enemy is hungry, feed him; if he is thirsty, give him something to drink. In doing this, you will heap burning coals on his head. Do not be overcome by evil, but overcome evil with good."*

Being under the altar signifies a place of close communion with God. The martyrs that are spoken of here were able to endure persecution and death at the hands of evil because of their close relationship with God. They spent time under the altar growing in intimacy with the Lord through worship, praise, prayer and His Word. How close to the altar are we?[8]

The Breaking Open of the Sixth Seal; Cosmic Signs:

This seal abruptly brings us back to the events on earth. There will be enormous cosmic disturbances occurring. For the ones living at that time, it may seem that the whole earth is coming apart. Verse 12 tells us that the earth quakes mightly, the sun turns black, the moon turns red (like blood). This could be a result of the atmospheric condition caused by the earthquakes. The *"sun turned black like sackcloth."* Now that's extreme. What is God saying?

Sackcloth was a coarse woolen fabric (usually black) worn by ancient Israelites as a symbol of mourning for the dead, or for a disaster, or for *repentance* (God's heart is that *all* repent). It also says the moon will look like blood. Joel 2:31 foretold:

> *"The sun shall be turned to darkness, and the moon to blood, before the great and awesome day of the Lord comes."*

Paul reminds of this again in Acts 2:20:

> *"The sun will be turned to darkness and the moon to blood before the coming of the great and glorious day of the Lord."*

I recently heard a pastor being interviewed about prophecies, and one thing in the interview stuck with me - "The Heavens are God's billboard to us." Old Testament prophets were able to read the skies and stars and hear from the Lord. From that they foretold signs and wonders. God is always speaking to us, but are we listening anymore? Jesus said it Himself in Luke 21:25, *"There will be signs in the sun, moon, and stars."*

I believe the Lord is lifting up people who are willing to seek Him and speak on His behalf to awaken us and prepare us. Pastor Don Finto is one of those people. He wrote a book recently that brings many current events to the forefront and cross references them with end time scriptures. This book helps bring to the forefront a need to be prepared. His book is titled *"Prepare! For The End Time Harvest"*[10]

I'm not trying to peddle others' books here, but the information is deep and when put against the truth of scripture, it is vital that we understand we are living in a very important time in history. Here's my point: this is a loving God we serve. He wants no one to perish. Yes, the end of this world is going to eventually come, but if we are seeking Him and heeding what He is saying to us, or has said to us through prophets, then why should we fear in terror? That type of fear is not of the Lord. Terror does not come from heaven. A reverent fear of who He is in all His majesty brings about wisdom. Proverbs 9:10 declares, *"The fear of the Lord is the beginning of wisdom, and knowledge of the Holy One is understanding."* During these changing times of uncertainty, wouldn't you want wisdom and understanding too?

Continuing on with 6:13, it mentions that the *"stars fall from the sky,"* describing it like figs falling off of a fig tree when a strong wind comes. Even the sky seems altered, *"receded like a scroll, rolling up."* In the land, every mountain and island will be removed from its place. For all of them to be moved from their place would indicate a geological catastrophe of gigantic proportions. Fear and flight are the reactions of the people who don't understand or are not prepared. These terrifying events prompt a three-fold response from all the unbelievers, identified in verse 15 as, *"Kings of the earth, princes, generals, the rich, the mighty, and every slave and free man…"* They instinctively hide themselves *"among the rocks of the mountains"* (probably caves). Their fear of God and the Lamb is so great, they call upon the rocks and the mountains to help them by falling on them to hide them from *"…the face of Him who sits on the throne and from the wrath of the Lamb."* (6:16) They fear the day of judgment.

What impact should the breaking of the seals have on our lives? The same impact God wanted for the seven churches of Asia Minor and all the Christians for the last 2,000 years. We must crown Jesus Christ as King of our lives!

When we watch a TV show for years, we may feel as though we know the people on the show. They feel like family and we may feel as though we know them. But do we really know them? No—there is no real relationship. The Great Tribulation will be a time of horrible distress, but knowing a lot about prophecy won't save you. Knowing about Jesus' life won't either. The only thing that will save you from all of this is a personal relationship with Jesus Christ. This happens by faith. Ask Him to be your Lord and Savior. Do it now, invite Him into your heart. Because on that day, *what* you know won't matter. The only thing that will matter is *Who* you know.[11]

Trust Him with not just your todays, but also your tomorrows. God's wrath is one of His eternal attributes, the perfect complement to His love. The wrath of God is His necessary and just response to sin.

> *"For God did not appoint us to suffer wrath but to receive salvation through our Lord Jesus Christ. He died for us so that, whether we are awake or asleep, we may live together with Him."*
>
> 1 Thessalonians 5:9-10

Endnotes:

1. http://www.gotquestions.org/threshing-floor.html#ixzz3fQjKCc8s
2. http://www.Biblestudytools.com/dictionary/threshing/
3. Community Bible Study Revelation Commentary by Timothy D. Crater, 1997-2004; Lesson 7, pg 1
4. Ibid., Lesson. 7, pg 2
5. Ibid., Lesson 7, pg 3
6. Kendall Easely, Revelation- Holman New Testament Commentary 1998 B & H Publishing Group; Nashville,TN; pg 108
7. Community Bible Study Revelation Commentary by Timothy D. Crater, 1997-2004; Lesson 7, pg 4
8. Community Bible Study Revelation Commentary by Phyllis Cooper, 1997-2004; Lesson 7, pg 5
9. PREPARE. For The End Time Harvest by Don Finto, copyright by Don Finto
10. Community Bible Study, TD Helps, 2008, Lesson 7, pg 21

CHAPTER 7

There is a scroll that has writing on both sides. This is God's judgments to the world. The scroll was rolled up and sealed with seven seals. We have reviewed six of them. The only thing keeping the scroll from falling open and the judgments being revealed, is the seventh seal.

There are people who are sealed in this chapter, so reading this chapter, it seems best to divide it into two parts; the "144,000" and the "Great Multitude."

The 144,000

This chapter begins with four angels restraining the wind. They are holding back the wind to prevent it from blowing anywhere *"on the land or the sea or on any tree."* On a hot day, even a small breeze is welcome. But these winds are not breezes at all. They are intended to harm the earth. As the four angels hold back the destructive winds, a fifth angel appears who calls out to the four other angels in 7:3:

> *"Do not harm the land or the sea or the trees until we put a seal on the foreheads of the servants of our God."*

Whatever kind of divine stamp or engraving he uses is really immaterial; all we know is that it is a spiritual seal, that will be recognized and honored by the destructive forces of God's creation – (which temporarily are being restrained by the four angels).[1] This is not to suggest that others are not sealed, but only that these servants are sealed and protected from the wrath of God. This would be similar to how God protected His people from the plagues and the angel of death, and ultimately from Pharaoh's army, in Exodus 9.

Commentator Ken Easley goes further:

"Ancient monarchs and officials often had engraved rings or

cylinders that were pressed on clay or wax to authenticate and protect what was sealed. Such a seal could be entrusted to a steward if it served the king's purposes. Here, this angel stamps God's seal "on the foreheads of the servants of our God" (7:3). This is similar to Ezekiel 9:3-4, "...Then the Lord called to the man clothed in linen who had the writing kit at his side and said to him, Go throughout the city of Jerusalem and put a mark on the foreheads of those who grieve and lament over all the detestable things that are done in it." There the mark was the Hebrew letter for T which was made like a plus sign or an X and was clearly literal. Here God's seal is almost certainly symbolic, for the ancient world did not know the practice of stamping the foreheads of individuals with a seal. Whether literal or not, it contrasts with the famous mark of the beast of Revelation 13:16."[2]

I'd like to point out that 144,000 is an exact and precise number. God knows the exact number of Gentiles chosen for salvation. Romans 11:25 says:

"I do not want you to be ignorant of this mystery, brothers and sisters, so that you may not be conceited: Israel has experienced a hardening in part until the full number of the Gentiles has come in."

He knows the exact number elected to martyrdom. Revelation 6:12 says:

"Then each of them was given a white robe, and they were told to wait a little longer, until the full number of their fellow servants, their brothers and sisters, were killed just as they had been."

As with these scriptures, we would expect Him to predetermine the exact number elected for this special sealing. Many have wondered, who are these 144,000? After reading several commentaries, I will offer some possible options:

1. Because of the listing of the tribes, some believe these are ethnic Jews.
2. Some say they are Christians.
3. Some say they are Messianic Jews.

I believe they are believers in Christ, who qualify as "servants of God" as stated in 7:3. It is quite possible that they are the tribulation Jews who are also believers in Christ.

Paul, also a Jew, referred to himself as a "servant of God" in Titus 1:1:

"Paul, of a servant God and an apostle of Jesus Christ to further the faith of God's elect and their knowledge of the truth that leads to godliness…"

This leads me to believe that these believers were Messianic Jews. Here are some other reasons I have come to this conclusion:

1. The church was founded by the Jewish Messiah.
2. His 12 apostles were also Jews,
3. As were most people in the early church.

Eventually, the church became predominantly Gentile. But God's purposes will soon turn again to the Jews and Israel, under its messianic King. These 144,000 Jews may well represent the beginning of that movement during the end times. With chapter 6, the opening of the seals brings about death and destruction, and in this chapter the angels have seals to protect life.

There are cults out there to have claimed the distinction of being the chosen 144,000. Everybody wants a sure thing. But we can't miss the point by focusing on this number. Our focus should be that all people who have received Jesus Christ as their Savior are - by faith - marked by God through the Holy Spirit. God's Spirit resides within each of us as our seal and a guarantee of eternal life.[3] This is a true hope that we must hold on to.

Regardless of what we believe about the Rapture - we have to come to terms that there will be Christian believers in the tribulation period. God loves them and protects them from His judgment, but as we shall see, they are subject to the same persecution and martyrdom that has always faced the church. And yet, remember Who it is we serve and remember this is not our home.

The Innumerable Gentile Saints:

Another larger group comes into focus next - *"a great multitude that no one could count."* (7:9)

Take a moment and just think about that. Can you imagine all those saints? Verse 14 says:

"These are they who have come out of the great tribulation."

These are Christians from every nation, tribe, people and language. They stand before the throne of God in white robes of righteousness that have been washed *"in the blood of the Lamb"* (7:14). They had been martyred and now they will forever stand before God worshiping and serving Him in glory. Hallelujah!

Paul summed it up best for us in Romans 8:8:

> *"I consider that our present sufferings are not worth comparing with the glory that will be revealed in us."*

That's the right perspective when thinking about going through the Tribulation. Our eyes have to be fixed on heaven and what awaits us there. God made promises to Israel, the nation, that must be preserved in order to be with Christ in His millennial Kingdom.

This all has to play out. This is God's plan and He hasn't forgotten us. He hasn't forgotten you.

No matter what we've gone through here on this earth, or what we might go through if left to live through the Tribulation, we should remember and hold dear to our hearts the last sentence in this chapter.

> *"And God will wipe away every tear from their eyes."*

Not some, but *every* tear.

Endnotes

1. Community Bible Study Revelation Commentary by Timothy D. Crater, 1997-2004; Lesson 8, pg 1
2. Kendall Easely, Revelation- Holman New Testament Commentary 1998 B & H Publishing Group; Nashville,TN; pg 125
3. Community Bible Study Revelation Commentary by Phyllis Cooper, 1997-2004; Lesson 8, pg 3

CHAPTER 8

THE OPENING OF THE SEVENTH SEAL
AND THE FOUR TRUMPET BLASTS

I've heard it said that judgment is a two sided coin: salvation for the faithful and punishment for the wicked. In the last few chapters we viewed the saved. Now another set of judgments are coming as the seventh seal is being opened. These judgments come as plagues and are introduced by angels blowing their trumpets. Tribulation is unfolding and John foresees these divine plagues. They are devastating and overwhelming. He sees a parallel to the plagues of ancient Egypt, yet on a worldwide scale. Again, there is a divine plan from the Lord.

Both sets of plagues are warnings; offering the ungodly a chance to repent.[1] This is always God's heart. He loves all of us, and He wants no one to perish. These judgments are part of His great plan, and His hope is that people will see that they need Him, that they will repent and live in eternity with Him. That's the goal. But that choice is up to us and God's plan still has to move forward regardless of what we decide.

Our contemporary society as a whole has, for the most part, very little knowledge of Scripture, wouldn't you say? Yet occasionally on the news, a reporter will describe a flood's devastation or a famine as being of "biblical proportions." To report disasters in this way makes me wonder what they'll say when reporting about the plagues and devastation that will take place. This is all according to God's ultimate plan before Christ's return.

God sent the original plagues (of truly Divine proportions) on Pharaoh and Egypt (found in the book of Exodus chapters 7-10). Those ten plagues/disasters that God sent, brought about the release of the nation of Israel from their bondage.[2]

There's a parallel here of God's motivation.

- Both sets of plagues are warnings that offer the ungodly an opportunity to repent.
- Both sets of plagues are divine judgments that go beyond any "natural" explanation.
- Both sets of plagues result in salvation and victory for the people of God.

Jesus, the Lamb, opens the seventh seal on the scroll. The scroll is opened and God reveals His end-time judgment on sin. Verse one reveals a dramatic pause. Silence is all around…no sound at all…for one-half hour. Think about this for a moment. God's heavenly creatures; the elders and angels, who have been praising Him continuously without ceasing from the beginning of their creation, now fall silent for perhaps for the first time…ever! This is the eerie calm before the storm.

I remember September 11, 2001 vividly. But I also recall that the United States had halted all flights in the sky that day after the attack on the twin towers. I remembered I walked outside later that day and realized that there was not one plane in the sky. It was all an eerie silence. I had no idea how conditioned I was to hearing a plane over head. I guess more often than I realized, I was used to hearing a plane or two fly overhead during each hour of the day - until this day. Now, that wasn't heaven, but the silence was quite noticeable and in fact eerie. I think about that moment in time and compare it to this moment in scripture here. Praise, worship, and all heavenly noise - falling silent - for a full half hour. It makes my hair stand up on the back of my neck.

Some commentators believe this silent time is a period of silence for the prayers of the saints to be heard. Other commentators believe it is time for the newly unrolled scroll to be read and directions for equipping the angels are given so they can be carried out.

Then in 8:3, we see an angel approach the altar carrying a golden censer (a fire pan used to hold smoldering charcoal that would burn the incense). After offering up the incense along with the prayers of the saints, he filled the censer with fire from the altar and hurled it to earth, followed by peals of thunder, rumblings, flashes of lightening and an earthquake! (8:5).

John didn't report the contents of the prayers. Perhaps they were the cries of the martyrs, *"How long Oh Lord?"* (from 6:10), and the Lord would say *"wait a little longer."* (6:11) Now the answer begins with the trumpet blast and the mood has changed from intercession to judgment. The unraveling of the world has begun.[3]

Trumpets have significance in Jewish history. The Feast of Trumpets celebrates the New Year and the giving of the Law at Mt. Sinai. The Israelites took the wall of Jericho down with the blast of their trumpet (a ram's horn called a Shofar). Watchmen stood on Jerusalem's walls and blew the trumpets to warn Israel of danger. Now we have angels blowing their heavenly trumpets announcing God's judgement on the sin of the world.

Ezekiel 33:6 says:

> *"But if the watchman sees the sword coming and does not blow the trumpet to warn the people and the sword comes and takes someone's life, that person's life will be taken because of their sin, but I will hold the watchman accountable for their blood."*

Just like the watchman on the wall, we have a responsibility to warn others as well. We must blow the trumpet and urge people to seek Christ now, while He can be found.[4]

The Angels and the Trumpets

In 8:6, seven angels stand poised with seven trumpets, which they prepare to blow.

At the sound of the first four trumpets, we see the beginning of God's wrath unleashed.

1. Hail and fire mixed with blood fall, burning up one-third of the earth. (8:7)
2. A huge mountain-like object is thrown into the oceans, turning one-third of them to blood, killing one-third of the sea creatures, and destroying one-third of the ships. (8:8-9)
3. A huge blazing star called Wormwood falls on one-third of the fresh waters, turning them bitter. (8:10-11)
4. And one-third of the sun, moon and stars are darkened, resulting in one-third less light on earth. (8:12)

I want to point out something to you regarding 8:12. Remember, God pledged to Noah that *"as long as the earth endures…day and night will never cease."* (Gen 8:22) I point this out because with just the sound of His mighty voice He could wipe it all away. After all, this holy God spoke it all into existence, so He can speak it into destruction with one word, right? But God chooses to keep His promises to us. Even through all of this, He still keeps His word.

God has given us a peek of what is to come through the prophet Joel.

> *"I will show wonders in the heaven and on the earth, blood and fire and billows of smoke."*

Joel 2:30

Commentators have written of different ways these things could happen (scientifically speaking), so let's spend a little time here on that.

> *"The first angel sounded his trumpet, and there came hail and fire mixed with blood, and it was hurled down on the earth. A third of the earth was burned up, a third of the trees were burned up, and all the green grass was burned up."*

Revelation 8:7

This could be a nuclear disaster, or even an asteroid strike. Either way this brings on a worldwide ecological catastrophe. It destroys land, it burns up trees which could provide shade, fruit and building materials.

In Exodus 9:24-26 God moved in a similar fashion:

> *"...hail fell and lightning flashed back and forth. It was the worst storm in all the land of Egypt since it had become a nation. Throughout Egypt hail struck everything in the fields—both people and animals; it beat down everything growing in the fields and stripped every tree. The only place it did not hail was the land of Goshen, where the Israelites were."*

With the earth's vegetation ruined, man's food supply is profoundly affected.[5] Notice how He spared His children.

> *"The second angel sounded his trumpet, and something like a huge mountain, all ablaze, was thrown into the sea. A third of the sea turned into blood, a third of the living creatures in the sea died, and a third of the ships were destroyed."*

Revelation 8:8-9

This may suggest a meteor of some kind. It burn up as it falls through earth's atmosphere and then into the sea. I came across an article once about a mountain-sized asteroid that they say almost hit the earth.[6]

The sea would change color to red because of the "fiery mountain" being hurled into it. It would kill marine life and it would disrupt shipping across the seas, which would deeply impact commerce, industry and even our food supply - not to mention the stench a few billion dead fish would produce. Nasty!

> *"The third angel sounded his trumpet, and a great star, blazing like a torch, fell from the sky on a third of the rivers and on the springs of water - the name of the star is Wormwood. A third of the waters turned bitter, and many people died from the waters that had become bitter."*
>
> Revelation 8:10-11

This could be a comet. Its dusty fallout would darken the sky and pollute the atmosphere and destroy the fresh waters of the world which mankind needs to survive. Wormwood, which in the Old Testament represents the judgment of God on disobedient people, is a class of bitter plants which were paired with "poisoned water." In Jeremiah 9:14-15 the Lord says:

> *"Instead, they have followed the stubbornness of their hearts; they have followed the Baals, as their ancestors taught them. Therefore this is what the Lord Almighty, the God of Israel, says: 'See, I will make this people eat bitter food and drink poisoned water.'"*

This seems a fitting name for a poisonous star/torch that falls on the earth's fresh waters.[7]

> *"The fourth angel sounded his trumpet, and a third of the sun was struck, a third of the moon, and a third of the stars, so that a third of them turned dark. A third of the day was without light, and also a third of the night."*
>
> Revelation 8:12

How this will happen is not stated. But it parallels the account in the book of Exodus, when Egypt was judged with a terrifying darkness, a darkness that could be felt.

> *"Then the Lord said to Moses, "Stretch out your hand toward the sky so that darkness spreads over Egypt - darkness that can be felt."*
>
> Exodus 10:21

When we consider how humanity depends on light for food, energy and daily living, we can appreciate the impact darkness might have on life.

These are just suggestions, but in any case these will be no ordinary meteorites or asteroids. I think it's important to note here that John is not concerned to provide information about *how* it happens, just that it is the hand of God that does it. I say this in case you start to get too anxious about how all of this plays out. We can only guess the *how*, but we can all agree it is by God's divine and powerful hand - and that's all we really need to know.

This is the beginning of His wrath. These trumpets are like a reveille call to *wake up*. They are a warning sound. Let me make this clear, God does not want His children to perish. We are His creation and His original design for us is life, not death. Ezekiel quotes the Lord here:

> *"As surely as I live, declares the Sovereign Lord, I take no pleasure in the death of the wicked, but rather that they turn from their ways and live. Turn."*

Ezekiel 33:11

The Lord is addressing Israel directly in this passage, but it might as well be all of us - Gentile or Jew. This is God's heart. But there is a sovereign plan for judgment; this is His will. And God's will, will be done.

The Angels

Let's talk about the angels that sound the trumpets. These angels are not the chubby little cherubs that we see in many displays or in people's home decor. These angels God created in holiness and gave them great power. In Psalms 1-3 and Psalm 91, Angels are *"mighty ones who do His bidding"* and *"guard us in all our ways."* Angels' jobs are also to warn and they can inflict punishment on individuals too. Their whole existence is to serve and honor God. They certainly aren't silly little cherubs, so get that image out of your head as you read on.

The Trumpets

The trumpet sounds are warnings. I want to pause for a second and point something out to you. These plagues that will come will be devastating, yes, but they are not fatal - not yet anyway. As severe as the first four trumpet judgments have been, the worst is yet to come. Verse 13 goes on to say an eagle (some translations ay a vulture) flies over.

The Greek word here is "aetos" which can refer to either bird. This creature flies or circles overhead, just waiting for the dead, and it cries: *"Woe, Woe, Woe!"* It might be saying:

- Woe! To earth dwellers and unbelievers…Woe to you.
- Woe! To the believers in Jesus Christ, it is time to get prepared.
- Woe! To all inhabitants of the earth.

One Third (1/3)

When the seals of the scrolls were opened (6:1-9), the first four were clustered together, each presenting a dreadful horseman. Here is the same pattern with the first four trumpets, each involving the fraction one-third. The word or fraction one-third is found 14 times in this chapter. The fraction represents *incompleteness*. All the "thirds" are demolished - earth, trees, sea marine life, shipping, rivers, springs, sun, moon, stars, day and night - are all are substantially damaged, but the damage is limited.

This is a time of severe, but still incomplete, judgment. The severity of it is why some scholars call this the *Great* Tribulation.

God also uses our five senses to get our attention:

- The sight of angels and blazing objects.
- The sound of trumpets and thunder.
- The smell of incense and smoke.
- The taste of bitter wormwood.
- The feel of an earthquake.[8]

Remember, God will use whatever means He can, even natural disasters, to accomplish His purposes. It's designed to bring people to repent. People often hear the gospel more clearly in the face of disasters.

I remember when I was a little girl, the emergency broadcast system would come on the radio or TV and say, "This is a test. In an actual emergency you must go to the nearest shelter." It was scary at times, especially as a child. But it was all designed (and still is) to protect and prepare people in case of an actual emergency.[9]

The Great Tribulation will be a time of great suffering and pain, and it *is* coming. But the Lord has given us a hope through all of it. Through His love for us He has provided shelter for us in His Son, Jesus Christ.

> *"Whoever believes in Him will not perish."*
>
> John 3:16

We must be a broadcast system to all who do not believe.

Endnotes:

1. Kendall Easely, Revelation- Holman New Testament Commentary 1998 B & H Publishing Group; Nashville,TN; pg 141
2. Ibid., pg.141
3. Ibid., pg 143
4. Community Bible Study Revelation Commentary by Phyllis Cooper, 1997-2004; Lesson 9, pg 2
5. Community Bible Study Revelation Commentary by Timothy Crater, 1997-2004; Lesson 9, pg 4
6. http://www.space.com/28371-asteroid-2004-bl86-earth-flyby.html
7. Community Bible Study Revelatoin Commentary by Timothy Crater, 1997-2004, Lesson 9, pg 5
8. Kendall Easely, Revelation- Holman New Testament Commentary 1998 B & H Publishing Group; Nashville,TN; pg 147
9. Community Bible Study TD Helps; 2008; Lesson 9; pg 25

CHAPTER 9

FIFTH TRUMPET AND FIRST WOE: THE LOCUST PLAGUE

U ntil this point, God has used forces of nature to wake up an unbelieving world. Now He's turning up the heat - using new instruments of extreme measure to get the attention of non-believers. Why? Because something extremely important is at stake - the souls of the unbelieving people. He is literally moving heaven and hell to keep them from perishing.

The fifth trumpet blows in verse one. An angel falling from the sky has the keys to the Abyss, and opens it. Some say this may be satan himself. No one knows for sure, but whoever it is, out of this abyss comes an evil empire of demonic creatures.

We see another evil empire described in the book of Joel, as it invades the land of Judah;

> *"What the locust swarm has left, the great locusts have eaten; what the locusts have left, the young locusts have eaten; what the young locusts have left, other locusts have eaten.*
>
> *Wake up, you drunkards, and weep. Wail, all you drinkers of wine; a nation has invaded my land, powerful and without number; it has the teeth of a lion, the fangs of a lioness.*
>
> *It laid waste my vines and ruined my fig trees. It has stripped off their bark and thrown it away, leaving their branches white.*

Joel 1:4-7

Here, the locusts are compared to a nation. During this time in history, Rome would consider the Parthian Empire to be the evil empire. The

Parthian warriors were fearsome. The Roman people expected the Parthian's to cross the Euphrates and attack Rome. They were regaining their independence after losing it to Alexander the Great. They were fierce and they were on the move. They're described as locusts because of the size of their armies and the military tactics they used to destroy the people and land. Here's a brief description of them:

> *Their steel armor often rusted and shone fiery red in the bright sunlight. In particular their bowmen in chariots were fierce, with the skill of shooting arrows both ahead and behind. Retreating from battle, their archers shot poisoned arrows over their shoulders causing the same effect as the poison of scorpion tails. According to some accounts, Parthian warriors wore long flowing hair, but twisted the tails of their horses into snake-like ropes.*[1]

This description is fierce, aggressive and somewhat evil. But remember, true evil comes out of the Abyss. Just imagine a huge underground cavern, like an old gold mine. Then imagine a narrow shaft going up to the surface, with a lock at the top. Now picture the cavern filled with choking blue smoke created by a sulfurous, crude-oil burning furnace.[2]

This angel opens the locked door at the top and the smoke would just belch up from the shaft, *"like the smoke from a gigantic furnace."* (9:2) In this instance, *"the sun and sky were darkened by the smoke"* (9:2) - an ominous pre-cursor of the real terrors that come from that pit.

These locust demons appear to be a special class of evil spirits that has remained under God's lock and key until this time.

God has locked up another group of spirits before. The book of Jude it tells us:

> *"And the angels who did not keep their positions of authority but abandoned their own home - these He has kept in darkness, bound with everlasting chains for judgment on the great Day."*
>
> Jude 6

I write this only to remind us again, that this is all orchestrated by God Himself. He is allowing the lock to be opened by this angel of authority. It only seems to the human eye that God has lost control and satan and his demonic forces are going to have a heyday. But, God is allowing this, because God is in charge of all of this. We must keep this in mind as we go through these chapters. This is why I continually remind you of this.

These locusts/scorpions come out like a military army and they have a leader, an arch-demon (this could be the same demon we'll read about in 11:7). His name is Abaddon, verse 11 tells us. This is a Hebrew term for, "a personification of destruction."[3]

Apollyon is mentioned also as the Greek name which still means, "destroyer."[4] Some commentaries say this is a slur toward the Greek god Apollo, who the Roman emperors worshiped, and perhaps that is why John put that in there. But we can only speculate on this.

If heaven's angels have different ranks and orders, then we should expect the same from the demonic world as well, right?

John uses strong words like agony, torture and suffering to explain what they will do to unbelievers. Verse six goes on to say:

> "During those days men will seek death, but will not find it; they
> will long to die, but death will elude them."

This is to get them to repent. God brought about some severe plagues and disasters on Pharaoh to soften his heart too. But sadly, then and even here, there will still be people who will not yield. This torture mentioned in 9:10 will last five months - the life span of a locust.

Have you ever had a child wander off in a public place, or saw them heading toward danger? I have heard of mothers literally lifting cars off of babies. A parent will do anything to find that child or save that child. Maybe you have a child or loved one that has run away from God? If you could, and you knew it was a matter of life and death, you would use extreme measures to get their attention to cause them to turn around, wouldn't you? It would be *because* you love them so much and don't want any harm to come to them.

These unbelievers are lost ones that are precious to our Heavenly Father. They are lost and in danger of being lost forever. He is using extreme measures to get their attention so they will turn toward Him. Time is running out! The clock is ticking. Judgment is coming. The door of heaven is closing soon. These are extreme measures of love for His lost ones. He is the true Shepherd going after His sheep. It gives you an idea of how much He loves us and doesn't want *anyone* to perish. That is love, true love. But sadly, not all will repent.

If the terrors of these creatures were so bad that men longed to die, we know with the second woe and trumpet sound this will bring events to an even worse place than before.

The Sixth Trumpet and the Second Woe

There's a voice from heaven that calls for the release of the four angels bound near the Euphrates (9:13). These angels are evil angels and have been kept for this very hour, day, month and year, scripture tells us in verse 15. Now unbound, they're commanded to kill one-third of all mankind. I think about those New Year's Eve clocks that countdown the time right down to the minute and second, and the seconds keep moving forward. It either brings on a feeling of excitement or anxiousness. But either way, time still moves forward.

Time is moving forward to bring about this moment too.

God's army of wrath is armed and prepared to go somewhere near the Euphrates. The mounted troops would number 200 million. For both the Israelites of the Old Testament and the Romans of the New Testament, hostile eastern armies were usually stopped by the Euphrates.[5] What John saw was demon armies of two hundred million troops marching over the Euphrates. It was not stopping them this time.

The focus is on the horse, not the rider, as it is described in 9:17:

Their breastplates were fiery red, dark blue, yellow as sulfur…
…heads of horses resembled heads of lions…
…out of their mouths came fire, smoke, and sulfur…
…their tails were like snakes, having heads with which they inflict injury…

Now go back and read about the Parthian Warriors that were described earlier. This is similar to the scary and fierce description of them. You can see now how things could fall into place with these types of descriptions.

This army will kill over two billion people, yet after the smoke clears (literally, fire and brimstone), there will still be those who still won't repent. These survivors have lived through earthquakes, conquest, famine, disasters, locusts from hell, and all this death, but still will not see. Why? What is so important to them? 9:20-21 gives us the answer:

"The rest of mankind who were not killed by these plagues still did not repent of the work of their hands; they did not stop worshiping demons, and idols of gold, silver, bronze, stone and wood - idols

that cannot see or hear or walk. Nor did they repent of their
murders, their magic arts, their sexual immorality or their thefts."

People don't want to give up their money, their sex or their drugs. These offer an illusion of fulfillment. Apart from Jesus, this is the best the world can offer. They love their idols more than God Himself. That's why Jesus needs to be the center of it all - all the time - and every day.

C. S. Lewis, in his book "The Screwtape Letters," brings up an interesting point:

> *"There are two equal and opposite errors into which our race can*
> *fall about the devils. One is to disbelieve in their existence. The*
> *other is to believe, and to feel an excessive and unhealthy interest*
> *in them. They themselves are equally pleased by both errors, and*
> *hail a materialist or a magician with the same delight."*

We shall see this interest increase as the days approach us. Just look at all the increased interest in the occult. Vampire movies and TV shows, demons, witches, magic, etc…

The second Commandment tells us that we should have no other gods before Him. Yet, we make these things more important than our relationship with God. John warns us about how people will be and act, but he also gives us guidance how to not be deceived.

> *"Dear friends, do not believe every spirit, but test the spirits to see*
> *whether they are from God, because many false prophets have gone*
> *out into the world. This is how you can recognize the Spirit of God:*
> *Every spirit that acknowledges that Jesus Christ has come in the*
> *flesh is from God, but every spirit that does not acknowledge Jesus*
> *is not from God. This is the spirit of the antichrist, which you have*
> *heard is coming and even now is already in the world. You, dear*
> *children, are from God and have overcome them, because the One*
> *who is in you is greater than the one who is in the world."*

John 4:1-4

Peter reminds us:

> *"Be self-controlled and alert. Your enemy the devil prowls around*
> *like a roaring lion looking for someone to devour."*

1 Peter 5:8

God's clock is running; the countdown is in progress - counting down the years, months, days, hours, minutes and seconds. Time goes by quickly. Some people live their lives in unbelief, because they think they have time. To them, death or tribulation seems far away. But the truth is, they don't.

Earlier during the five-month locust plague, the king of the Abyss had only the power to torment. Now these four evil angels and their armies will kill/murder one-third of mankind. At today's population level that totals approximately two *billion* lives lost. Maybe even more. People who are dying never say, "I wish I had more money, drank more beer and had more sex." Instead they wish they had loved God and their family more. These are the eternal things that matter. Paul said in 1 Corinthians 13:13:

> *"And now these three remain: faith, hope and love. But the greatest of these is love."*

God loves you and He wants to spend eternity with you. Invite Him into your life. Stop everything and do this right now. Don't waste another moment gambling with your eternal destination.

> *My prayer for you is this: "But the Lord is faithful, and He will strengthen and protect you from the evil one. May the Lord direct your hearts in to God's love and Christ's perseverance."*
>
> 2 Thessalonians 3:3, 5

Endnotes:

1. http://www.iranchamber.com/history/parthians/parthian_army.php   and Kendall Easely, Revelation- Holman New Testament Commentary 1998 B & H Publishing Group; Nashville,TN; pg 158
2. Kendall Easely, Revelation- Holman New Testament Commentary 1998 B & H Publishing Group; Nashville,TN; pg 157
3. The NIV Study Bible, Copyright 1985 by The Zondervan Corporation
4. Community Bible Study Revelation Commentary by Timothy Crater, 1997-2004, Lesson 10, pg 4
5. Kendall Easely, Revelation- Holman New Testament Commentary 1998 B & H Publishing Group; Nashville,TN; pg 160
6. Ibid., pg 160
7. "The Screwtape Letters" by C. S. Lewis, Published by HarperOne; Ill Dlx edition, pg 3

CHAPTER 10

ny good coach knows the value of time-outs in a game. They should not be wasted, and are most effective and powerful when used in the final seconds of a game. In those "time-out" moments, the coach communicates with his players, calms them down, reassures them, reminds them of the game plan and gives special instructions for carrying that plan out.[1]

In this chapter, during the middle of the Great Tribulation, God calls a time-out to give His people reassurance and hope that He will carry out His plan, and to remind them that He is still very much in control.

There has already been an earlier pause, or time-out, that occurred in chapter 7, before the final seal was opened. Chapter 10 records another time-out before moving into end time judgments. This pause gives us time to consider some positive aspects of God's work before the counting of the woes resumes in Revelation 11:14.[2]

The Mighty Angel

We see a mighty angel appear at this point in 10:1 who comes in Christ's name. Some believe that this is Christ Himself, because the description is so similar to the description of Christ in the first chapter of Revelation. But John does not worship this angel, and the oath spoken in verse 10:6 is peculiar if this is indeed Christ Himself.

> "And he swore by him who lives forever and ever who created the heavens and all that is in them..."

Since you typically don't swear on yourself, this is more likely an angel that comes in Christ's name. Let's say, just for the sake of argument, this could be the angel Gabriel, who also stands in the very presence of God. Some people believe this. In Luke 1:19 it says:

> *"And the angel answered, 'I am Gabriel. I stand in the presence of God, and I have been sent to speak to you…'"*

The mighty angel of Revelation 10:5-6 is similar to Gabriel as described, and also in Daniel's vision in 12:7. Let's look:

- Revelation 10:5-6: *"Then the angel I had seen standing on the sea and on the land raised his right hand to heaven. And he swore by him who lives forever and ever, who created the heavens and all that is in it, and the sea and all that is in it, and said, 'There will be no more delay.'"*
- Daniel 12:7: *"The man clothed in linen, who was above the waters of the river, lifted his right and his left hand toward heaven, and I heard him swear by him who lives forever, saying, 'It will be for a time, times and half a time…'"*

No one can be sure, but this comparison was too much fun to pass up. Whether or not this *powerful* angel was Gabriel isn't really important, What is important is that he proclaims God's dominion over the earth.

The Seven Thunders

The Old Testament compared God's voice to a thunderstorm. Psalm 29:3 says:

> *"The voice of the Lord is over the waters; the God of glory thunders over the mighty waters."*

In this Psalm, which speaks of such might and power from our God, it is worthy to note that *"the voice of the Lord"* is used seven times. Again, seven equals completeness. God doesn't do anything by accident. In John 12:29, it says:

> *"The crowd that was there and heard it said it had thundered."*

Whatever the seven thunders are here, they speak directly for God. John does not explain, but it is clear that he understood what the thunderous voices were saying because he was forbidden to write it down. What the voice said is that it will happen in God's perfect and appropriate time. Daniel was given a similar order, which is recorded in Daniel 12.

Deuteronomy 29:29 says:

> *"The secret things belong to the Lord our God."*

When Paul was shown parts of heaven he said he -*"heard inexpressible things, things that man is not permitted to tell."*

2 Corinthians 12:2-4

Clearly God will reveal to us in due time what His plan is. We must trust we'll know when God is ready for us to know.

Then, in 10:6, the angel swears an oath to those in the Tribulation that there will be no more delay. When the seventh angel sounds the seventh trumpet, the mystery of God will be accomplished and the trumpet sound initiates the final events to come. What the prophets of the Old Testament have seen will now be fulfilled.

I found this commentary that makes some excellent points, and I want to share it with you.

> *"With the 'thunders' statement sealed up, John turns back to the mighty angel astride land and sea. He sees him raise "his right hand to heaven," and swear an oath. First, he declares God's eternal existence: "by Him who lives forever and ever." He then affirms God's role as Creator, "who created heaven and all that is in them, the earth and all that is in it, and the sea and all that is in it."(10:6). The substance of the oath is simple and straightforward: "there will be no more delay." God focuses John on the importance of the seventh trumpet judgment, saying that in the days when it is about to sound, "the mystery of God will be accomplished.(10:7)"*

The back will break on the world, its ways, and its system - making way for the Second Coming of Jesus Christ. Speculation is pointless for us as to when this will happen, but God, our God, the One in control, knows the day and the hour. Even right down to the minute and second.

The Little Scroll

In 10:9-10, John asked for the scroll from the angel, as he was instructed to do. He was commanded to eat it. It would taste first sweet, then sour. God's message to us brings both joy and sorrow. The prophets being compelled to announce God's judgment upon others not only experienced the sweetness, but the sourness as well.

When we go deeper with our understanding of scripture, pondering and internalizing it, we can in some ways look at this as chewing and swallowing it to live in us like John did. We know that in this fallen world, as it gets worse (and it will get worse), we will need the Word of God, which is the truth, to get us through. As it becomes a part of us, it becomes entrusted to us as well. We will want and need to proclaim it to others. This will be both a blessing and a burden. It will cause separation among friends and maybe even family. That's the sour part. It's possible that we may be martyred for our own stance on truth because of this prophecy. And even though we know that the martyred are considered faithful and have a great glory that awaits them in heaven, these are still not happy prospects for John, or any believer to contemplate. Yet again, our focus is directed not at our lives here, but on our eternal life with Christ who is in heaven.

Verse 11 states:

> "Then I was told, 'You must prophesy again about many people, nations, languages and kings.'"

This indicates that it has worldwide implications. The prophecy deals with the fate of the *whole* human race, not just with one nation. Indeed, Revelation concerns the fate of the *whole world*.

Remember the hymn "Turn Your Eyes Upon Jesus?" That refrain has lots of truth for us as we live in today's world. Current events can easily point us to end time prophecies possibly being fulfilled even now - and that can be downright scary. But if we focus our hearts and minds on Jesus Christ, then the things of this world really don't matter as much. It's a beautiful hymn that should help bring comfort to you when doubt and fear prey on you. The chorus to the song is:

Turn your eyes upon Jesus
Look full in His wonderful face
And the things of this world will grow strangely dim
In the light of His glory and grace [4]

Endnotes:

1. Community Bible Study TD Helps; 2008; Lesson 11; pg 32
2. Kendall Easely, Revelation- Holman New Testament Commentary 1998 B & H Publishing Group; Nashville,TN; pg 173
3. Engaging God's Word: Revelation, Copyright 2012 by Community Bible Study
4. "Turn Your Eyes Upon Jesus" by Helen H. Lemmel, 1922, Pubic Domain

CHAPTER 11

hapter 11 begins with John's order to measure the temple and its altar, as well as to count the worshipers there. Interpreters differ on the identity of the temple.

- Some suggest it symbolizes the Church.
- Some suggest it symbolizes Israel.
- Some take this as a literal temple in the tribulation period.

I'm inclined to believe that there are factors that suggest it very well may be a literal temple.[1]

Here's why:

The Lord Himself cited Daniel's prophecy about the end times in Daniel 9:27, that there will be an earthly temple in Jerusalem prior to His Second coming. The antichrist will stand there, so this must be a physical place. Let's look at some scripture references:

- Matthew 24:15 - *"So when you see standing in the holy place 'the abomination [the antichrist] that causes desolation,' spoken through the prophet Daniel - let the reader understand..."*
- 2 Thessalonians 2:4 - *"He will oppose and will exalt himself over everything that is called God or is worshiped, so that he sets himself up in God's temple, proclaiming himself to be God."*
- Daniel 9:27 - *"He will confirm a covenant with many for one 'seven.' In the middle of the 'seven' he will put an end to sacrifice and offering. And on a wing of the temple, he will set up an abomination that causes desolation, until the end that is decreed is poured out on him.'*[2]

If the antichrist stops sacrifices and grain offerings - this presumes a resumption of the Jewish sacrificial system and temple worship, this may very well indicate that there will be a literal temple. Jerusalem comes into focus more as it is also called the holy city in 11:2. The Greek word John uses for temple is "naos" which refers to the inner sacred areas.[3]

The measuring that John is told to do would suggest God's particular interest in the temple, the altar and the counting of the worshipers. This would imply that they will be protected, while the unmeasured part, the outer court, is given over to being trampled by the Gentiles.[4]

The prophet Zechariah had a vision of a man with a measuring line and that vision was about the full restoration and blessing for His people, His temple and His city.

> *"Then I looked up, and there before me was a man with a measuring line in his hand. I asked, 'Where are you going?' He answered me, 'To measure Jerusalem, to find out how wide and how long it is.' While the angel who was speaking to me was leaving, another angel came to meet him and said to him: 'Run, tell that young man, Jerusalem will be a city without walls because of the great number of people and animals in it. And I myself will be a wall of fire around it, declares the Lord, 'and I will be its glory within.'"*

Zechariah 2:1-5

The 42-month trampling by the Gentiles in 11:2, most commentators believe, is referring to the last three and a half years of the seven year Tribulation. After making a treaty with Israel for seven years, the antichrist breaks it halfway through, and puts an end to the temple offerings. This is found in the vision the Lord gave Daniel in 9:27:

> *"He will confirm a covenant with many for one 'seven.' In the middle of the 'seven' he will put an end to sacrifice and offering. And at the temple he will set up an abomination that causes desolation, until the end that is decreed is poured out on him."*

As he sets himself up as God - the abomination in the holy place - things will seem to get brutal in the outer court.

Just think how tense things will be when this happens. For example, the Temple Mount area in Jerusalem is home to the Jewish faith, the Muslim faith and the Christian faith. But if scripture is to be fulfilled, the "naos," the inner sacred place John refers to in 11:2 and that I mentioned earlier, would *have* to exist.

How can the temple be re-built? Today, *The Temple Institute in Jerusalem* exists because of a desire to rebuild their temple. According to them, there is a way to build without disturbing either of the two Muslim mosques currently standing on the site. They have a website where they solicite donations to make this become a reality. We very well may see in our lifetime the temple being rebuilt in Jerusalem. My point here is to show you that the possibility exists! Just Google this and see for yourself.[5]

The Two Witnesses

Scripture is truth. God's Word never comes back void. He is following His own rules He set for us to follow.

- Deuteronomy 17:6 - *"On the testimony of two or three witnesses a person is to be put to death, but no one is to be put to death on the testimony of only one witness."*
- 1 Timothy 5:19 - *"Do not entertain an accusation against an elder unless it is brought by two or three witnesses."*

This may answer why there were two witnesses. God was charging Israel and the Church with serious offenses and He sent forth two witnesses to bring their behavior to the surface through their preaching and their prophecies. This is designed to encourage people to repent and turn back to God. This lasts three and a half years, until 11:7 says, *"when they have finished their testimony."*

These two witnesses are like well-fueled lamps from God to a dark earth.[6] God provides them protection because they will need it. Given the severe evil on the earth during these times, many will try to harm them (11:5). But they will be more than a match for any foes.

11:5 says:

"fire will come from their mouths."

and verse 6 says they will *also* have the power to:

- dry up the sky while prophesying.
- change water into blood.
- strike the earth with every kind of plague - as often as they want.

Most commentators agree these two witnesses seem to be Elijah and Moses, or ones just like them.

- Elijah is known as the prophet by God's authority, called fire down from heaven. (2 Kings)

- Moses, through God's help, sent plagues to Pharaoh and changed water into blood. (Exodus)
- Both did not actually "die." At least, there is no biblical record of their deaths. They appear to have just been taken to heaven.[7]

It is easy to see why we should think that this may be Elijah and Moses coming back to speak truth for God. But this is only speculation. In John 7:7, John quotes Jesus' words:

"The world hates Me because I testify that what it does is evil."

The world will hate the two witnesses for the same reason it hated Jesus Christ. As the world grows darker, hatred of the light (which is Christ's light within us), will grow stronger. Nonetheless, the light must be held up because the light is the only hope for darkness.

The Mission of the Two Witnesses

These two witnesses are sent from God and speak for God, and their power comes from God. In 11:3, God calls them *"My two witnesses."* As I said earlier, they will have a powerful witness on earth. They will be able to do supernatural things on behalf of God. The ministry of these two witnesses only lasts 1,260 days (3 ½ years). This is probably the first half of the seven-year tribulation period since the antichrist will stop them. They are martyred/killed by the antichrist, who is *"the beast that comes up from the Abyss."*(11:7)

The Death of the Two Witnesses

God has marked out the days of their witness and He will grant the antichrist power over them for His sovereign purposes. It will seem like all is lost, but it is not. God is orchestrating all of this. He is in complete control.

The witnesses' bodies will be left in the street. This is such an indignity to all Jews! By being left unburied in the streets of Jerusalem, we can assume that this is their ministry location. When the two witnesses *"have finished their testimony"* (11:7), the antichrist will establish his 42-month reign of evil in Jerusalem. This is a dark time for all believers.

The city of Jerusalem is figuratively called *Sodom* and *Egypt* in 11:8. Why? Because it is:

- Hostile to the true people of God. This is why it is called Egypt.

- A hotbed of moral decadence. This is why it is referred to as Sodom.

Also this is where the Lord was crucified (11:8) and it confirms that John indeed means literal Jerusalem and that the witnesses are believers in Christ.

For three and a half days, there will be an international celebration over their deaths, from every people, tribe, language and nation. It gives us an idea of how effective the two witnesses' ministry will be. Scripture says that they will have tormented those who live on the earth. (11:10) Evil does not co-exist with good, so the truth that the witnesses speak over the world, will torment those who are following the evil ways of the enemy.

Even though they are based out of Jerusalem, their impact is worldwide. This is probably through the impact of cable and all the social media outlets. We are all globally connected today. These "gawkers" that want to see these dead bodies it seems, will flood into Jerusalem.

People are lost in darkness to the point that they will celebrate their deaths by exchanging gifts like it was Christmas. But this is an anti-Christmas. It's insanity! Having killed the messengers, they think they have killed the message and they can resume sinning.

Well, not quite. The God who reigns in heaven, rains on their parade.[8] God sends life back into the two witnesses, and they stand upright and crash this party! Can you imagine the look of terror on everyone's faces?

As the two witnesses ascend into heaven, God then sends an earthquake that takes out a tenth of the houses and buildings, resulting in the deaths of 7,000 people.

To some this serves as a wakeup call, because in 11:13 it says, in their terror, *"they gave glory to God of heaven."* We see once again, God is using any means to get His children's attention and to call them to repentance. He understands better than we do what eternal separation from His holy love really is, and because of that love, He will do whatever it takes to prevent that separation.

The Seventh Trumpet and the Third Woe

Let's review for a moment: The first woe (the fifth trumpet) was the locust plague from the Abyss; the second woe (the sixth trumpet) was the demonic army of the four unbound angels at the Euphrates. There has been a lengthy pause that has brought forth a powerful angel and the two witnesses. Now the seventh trumpet sounds and the focus is on the events that happen in heaven.

- There is a declaration of voices exclaiming *"the kingdom of the world has become the kingdom of our Lord and of His Christ, and He will reign forever and ever."* (11:15).
- The worship of the 24 elders who fall face down and give thanks and praise and worship to the Lord (11:16-18).

Following the trumpet sound is the opening of the temple of heaven and the appearance of the Ark of the Covenant. The ark was the most sacred symbol of God's covenant at Mt. Sinai with the sons of Abraham, and was placed within the holiest place of all in the temple. Above the ark, the very glory of God had appeared.[9]

This heavenly scene is a reminder that God has not forgotten His promises to Israel. They were set apart for Him and we as Gentiles were grafted in through Jesus Christ. We are His forever. With a New Jerusalem appearing, it is combining in a unique way the old and new covenants with Israel and the church.

As we see the temple of heaven, there are *"...flashes of lightning, rumblings, peals of thunder, an earthquake and a great hailstorm."*(Revelation 11:19)

Here in heaven, God is revealing more of His love and peace, reminding us all that He has not forgotten us and indeed wants us to be with Him in eternity. Are you beginning to see just how much He really loves us…all of us?

This is the bright spot in all this judgment. God's throne room is real, and He wants us there with Him!

Trust in God's promises for you.

Endnotes:

1. Community Bible Study Revelation Commentary by Timothy Crater, 1997-2004, Lesson 13, pg 1
2. Ibid., pg 1
3. Community Bible Study Revelation Commentary by Phyllis Cooper, 1997-2004, Lesson 13, pg 2
4. Community Bible Study Revelation Commentary by Timothy Crater, 1997-2004, Lesson 13, pg 1
5. https://www.templeinstitute.org/
6. Community Bible Study Revelation Commentary by Timothy Crater, 1997-2004, Lesson 13, pg 2
7. Ibid., pg 3
8. Ibid., pg 4
9. Ibid., pg 7

Chapter 12

As we study Revelation, we find much to think about concerning the new heaven and the new earth. These next chapters are viewed from a heavenly perspective, which is God's perspective. If you think about it, the Bible is the complete story of His love and plan for redemption from beginning to end. But the Bible is also a story of much conflict and war too. That's because from Genesis chapter 3 until the last two chapters of Revelation (chapters 21-22), God's enemy (and our enemy), satan, has been waging war against God, His people on earth, and in His heavenly realm.

In this chapter John is given the big picture overview of the great war. These are also the last desperate and malicious acts of satan.

The War on Earth and in Heaven

In Genesis 37, Joseph has a dream in which his father Jacob, his mother Rachel, and his eleven brothers are represented by *"the sun and moon and eleven stars."* John's vision in Revelation is a variation of this same theme for the woman (who represents the whole nation of Israel, not just Jacob's wife). She is *"clothed with the sun, with the moon under her feet and a crown of twelve stars on her head."* (12:1) The 12 stars represent the 12 tribes of Israel. Sun and moon equal heaven and light, and the woman (Israel) is in labor.

If you think about it, all of the Old Testament is about Israel's pregnancy as they wait for the Messiah to be born. Just think of the woman as the nation of Israel.[1]

> *"As the pregnant woman approaches the time to give birth, She writhes and cries out in her labor pains..."*
>
> Isaiah 26:17

"Writhe and labor to give birth, daughter of Zion - like a woman in childbirth…"

Micah 4:10

The Dragon Tries to Devour the Baby at Birth

In Matthew 2, we learn that King Herod had sent out a decree to have all male infants killed in Bethlehem. Joseph and Mary flee to Egypt to be safe - just as the vision revealed.

God preserves the woman (Israel) in the desert. God will also preserve Israel for the last half of the Tribulation, which is three and a half years. This is the generation of Jews living in Israel, particularly Jerusalem, during the last days, and of whom Jesus spoke from His message in Matthew 24-25. This desert place is her divine provision, like it says in 12:6, *"prepared for her by God."* These are the days that will follow the emergence of the antichrist and his murder of the two witnesses. They will coincide with his three and a half years of abuse of the outer court and the holy city which is mentioned in 11:1-2.[2]

The Dragon

There is little doubt that the dragon is satan himself. He is first described in 12:3 as - *"an enormous red dragon"* – perhaps suggesting his great power and bloodthirsty brutality.

The Head

In 11:3 the dragon is described as having seven heads, 10 horns and seven crowns. This represents the form that satan's power will take on in the Tribulation. This is similar to the vision of the end time events that Daniel received in chapter 7.

He sees a fourth and final powerful beast with 10 horns and another horn, a little one, arising and uprooting three of the first horns. Daniel 7:7-8 says:

> *"After that, in my vision at night I looked, and there before me was a fourth beast—terrifying and frightening and very powerful. It had large iron teeth; it crushed and devoured its victims and trampled underfoot whatever was left. It was different from all the former beasts, and it had ten horns. While I was thinking about the horns, there before me was another horn, a little one, which came up among them; and three of the first horns were uprooted*

before it. This horn had eyes like the eyes of a human being and a mouth that spoke boastfully."

An angel interprets this dream for him and tells him the 10 horns are 10 kings, and the little horn is another king (antichrist) who will *"subdue three of the kings."*[8] In Daniel 7:24, the angel explains the vision further:

"The ten horns are ten kings who will come from this kingdom. After them another king will arise, different from the earlier ones; he will subdue three kings."

If the antichrist emerges as one of the ten, but devours three others (that is, incorporates them into his own kingdom), the result is seven kingdoms and seven crowns, as described in 12:3. John's vision parallels that of Daniel's and confirms this as a political alliance of a Gentile world power dominated by satan and the antichrist.[3]

The Great War

Continuing with the story of the Great War, it seems before the dragon can devour the baby, in 12:5, the royal Son escapes into heaven. The dragon has missed out to complete his mission to destroy the heir and the woman flees to the desert, where God has made a place of protection for her. At this point, half way through the Tribulation, Michael the Archangel, the protector of God's people, and His angels wage war against satan and his demons. Michael prevails, and satan is cast out of heaven forever. Heaven is finally purged of him.

After the fall of Adam and Eve due to the serpent's cunningness, God speaks of the consequences of the fall in Genesis 3:15. This is the 'expanded version:'

"I will make you and the woman enemies to each other. Your descendants and her descendants will be enemies. One of her descendants will crush your head, and you will bite his heel."

Genesis 3:15 (EXB)

Although satan would strike Christ's heel (the Crucifixion), Christ will crush satan's head.

We now understand the Old Testament in a new way when we realize that satan's goal has been to destroy the Messianic line so that the Messiah could not defeat him at the cross. Let's look at some examples:

- Cain murdered Abel (so God replaced Abel's "good"

generational line with Seth).

- Pharaoh tried to wipe out the Israelites in Egypt (and God allowed them to escape).
- Saul tried to murder David (and God preserved David's life).
- At one point in Israel's history the continuation of the royal line rested on one little boy, Joash (see 2 Kings 11:1-21).
- God preserved Judah through the exile (and restored her to her land).[4]

Jesus Christ did come. He did die for us and was raised victorious. He *is* coming again. God's plans never fail! The dragon is doomed. We can count on that.

There are beliefs out there that God is finished with Israel because they rejected the Messiah. But this is simply *not* true. God made a covenant with them, a promise that will never be broken (Genesis 17). God is sinless and perfect, therefore we can be assured that He will keep His promises.

God is committed to preserving the Jewish nation. Just look at what He told Jeremiah to say to His people:

> *"This is what the LORD says, He who appoints the sun to shine by day, who decrees the moon and stars to shine by night, who stirs up the sea so that its waves roar - the LORD Almighty is His name. Only if these decrees vanish from My sight, declares the LORD, 'will the descendants of Israel ever cease to be a nation before Me.'"*

Jeremiah 31:35-36

Wow! Now that's a promise.

Yet, we know the enemy hates them, which is us, *God's people* - especially His original Covenant people *the Jews*. Here's an example of their history:

- They have been persecuted by Egypt, Babylon and Rome.
- They were driven out of Spain in the 1400's, and persecuted during the Crusades.
- They were placed in ghettos in Europe during the middle ages.
- They were killed and massacred by Poland and Russia in the 1800's.
- In Nazi Germany, six million Jews were murdered.
- Currently they are fiercely threaten by Iran and other middle

eastern countries.

Yet today, Israel survives. Why? Because of God's promise in Jeremiah 31! God is preserving His nation.[5]

Our enemy, satan, and his banishment from heaven is good news for them, but bad news for earth. Scripture is clear that as time draws closer to an end, satan will make things worse. He is not only furious, but clever. He wants us to do the opposite of things that we know will give us victory. For example:

- Fighting him in our own power.
- Destroying our testimony through moral failure.
- Clinging to this life and storing up our treasures here.

This kind of spiritual battle that we experience here is a foretaste of the battle to come in the last half of the Tribulation.

God does not want us ignorant. He has given us this book of Revelation for a reason. He wants us to live our daily lives in the context of His coming. You can't do that if you don't know what the Word of God says, so I encourage you to get into a Bible study. Learn about the promises of God and pay attention to what is going on around you. Seek the Holy Spirit's guidance. Recognize when there's temptation around you. We have the power to overcome satan.

James 4:7 says:

> *"Submit yourselves then to God. Resist the devil, and he will flee from you."*

Endnotes:

1. Community Bible Study Revelation Commentary by Timothy Crater, 1997-2004, Lesson 14, pg 1
2. Ibid,, pg 5
3. Ibid., pg 3
4. Community Bible Study Revelation Commentary by Phyllis Cooper, 1997-2004, Lesson 14, pg 4
5. Community Bible Study TD Helps; 2008; Lesson 14; pg 37

CHAPTER 13

In the seven-year Tribulation, satan unveils his last deception, his ultimate weapon of destruction - a man who will be the embodiment of everything evil, who will try to force the world to worship him. This is the dragon's strategy; to use this man as a prominent world leader. This man is known as the antichrist, a child of the Abyss, the seed of satan.[1] He will be a powerful world ruler that will rise quickly and with great authority.

The word 'antichrist' appears four times in the New Testament. (1 John and 2 John) In the Greek, the prefix *anti-* has several meanings; "against," "instead" or "in place of."

When used in Scripture, it could mean a person against Christ or a person instead of Christ - an imposter, a false Christ. The beast in this chapter is just that - a false Christ. He is the complete opposite of Jesus in every way.

The Beast from the Sea - (the antichrist)

To the Jews of the Old Testament, the sea was at times a symbol of evil and wickedness.

> *"But the wicked are like the tossing sea, which cannot rest, whose waves cast up mire and mud."*
>
> Isaiah 57:20

> *"They are wild waves of the sea, foaming up their shame; wandering stars, for whom blackest darkness has been reserved forever."*
>
> Jude 13

In Revelation 17:15, an angel says to John:

"The waters you saw...are peoples, multitudes, nations and languages."

The antichrist is coming out of the Abyss (11:7), that is, the evil ocean depths. One commentator said it this way:

"It is likely that he [satan] arises from that great Gentile sea of unrepentant humanity."[2]

The description of this dragon in 13:1, is similar to that in 12:3, which describes him as having seven crowns on seven heads and 10 horns. This time the beast is wearing 10 crowns - this is a look at end-time government powers forming a coalition or confederation and being headed up by the antichrist. His power and authority are given to him by the dragon. Daniel 7 and Revelation 17 say that the ten horns refer to ten kings.

In Daniel 7, Daniel had a vision that dealt with this end-time coalition that would begin with ten nations and be reduced to seven nations (when the little horn, or antichrist, uproots three nations and swallows them into his own kingdom). Because the antichrist is the premier ruler of this coalition, this multi-national beast represents him, (just as the Queen of England represents the British Commonwealth).

There will remain only seven heads, but they will represent ten dominions or countries (or crowns) and will wield the authority of ten states or governments (the horns.)[3] The blasphemous names on each of the heads would suggest a claim to a divine status or a god-like status. The body parts of this monster are a composite of three of the four creatures from Daniel 7:1-6, but in reverse order:

- The body of a leopard (suggests rapid and agile movement).
- The feet of a bear (implies long sharp claws for slashing prey).
- The mouth of a lion (suggests strong sharp fangs).

In Daniel's vision, these beasts represented historical empires that opposed Judah, such as Babylon and Persia. This is a formidable beast that moves quickly and widely. This is quite possibly a military power that is overwhelmingly destructive.[4]

Almost every passage that speaks of the antichrist emphasizes his boastful arrogant mouth as his most distinctive trait. His blasphemy will be aimed in three distinct directions:

- Against God Himself.
- Against heaven, God's dwelling place from which satan has been exiled.
- Against those who dwell in God's heaven.

He will verbally attack God and His heavenly associates and physically attack God's people on earth. Daniel saw this in the vision he was given.

"As I watched, this horn was waging war against the holy people and defeating them…"

Daniel 7:21

"He will speak against the Most High and oppress his holy people and try to change the set times and the laws. The holy people will be delivered into his hands for a time, times and half a time."

Daniel 7:25

Here's a point to ponder: The last world government was the Roman Empire; it brought enforced peace and stability, called the "Pax Romana." During the Tribulation, these are the two things the world will be hungry for, peace and stability. Instead of looking to God for this, the world will look to government and its ruler. This false god promises freedom, but gives bondage instead. The Tribulation will bring hopelessness to many who will not recognize what we are actually living through. In those times, the world will look to a charismatic leader to restore hope and give direction.

Do you think this can't happen? It's happened before. The late1930's were such a time. A worldwide depression brought hopelessness and despair. In Germany, one man rose up in the chaos, formed alliances, spoke with authority of a new world order (the Third Reich).

He waged an evil war against God's covenant people, set himself up as the total focus. He was almost "god-like," and he planned to rule the world while his countrymen praised him, shouting "Heil, Hitler!" Many faithful Christians who refused to bow down to his tyranny were put to death.

This is just one example where there was life promised, but instead death was delivered.

It's hard to think that this antichrist will rise to an even greater cruelty than that of Hitler. But remember, he, this anti-chirst, will be the embodiment of everything evil and Hitler will pale in comparison.[5]

The antichrist's Ascension

After the beast emerges from the sea, John gives us specific information about the antichrist's ascent to prominence through his head wound in 13:3.

The beast has seven heads, and represents seven rulers. One of them suffers an apparent fatal head wound. It is unclear whether this refers to a government's demise or to an actual human injury. In any case, the wound is healed and the world *is astonished.* (13:3) This miraculous healing of the head wound is so convincing that it provokes a worldwide reaction and the whole world *follows the beast.*

He is militarily unstoppable because they ask in 13:4, *"Who can make war against him?"* He is too powerful and mighty for any lesser king to challenge. This antichrist becomes satan's world ruler, who claims a divine status, and makes war on the saints.

The Beast from the Earth (The False Prophet)

Just as Moses had Aaron to speak for him, and Jesus had John the Baptist to prepare the way for Him, we now see the antichrist has a spokesman or prophet to enhance his false glory. He is the beast from the earth, and he too gets authority from satan.

The beast has two horns, scripture says. This equals power, but not kingship, as there is no crown. In verse 11 he acts *like a lamb* - soft and gentle, not harsh, yet he *speaks like a dragon.* He may use the church or a religion to seem holy and righteous. But the real source of his power is satan. False prophets have a false message: and that message is - *man is God.* That has been satan's lie from the beginning, because his goal is to take worship away from the true God. He will deceive many with his miracles, like the fire from heaven. (13:14)

Always know that God's Spirit draws no attention to Himself. Rather He points the world to Jesus Christ, bringing Him glory. This will always be the case. These people will be too gullible to know the truth, because their unbelief put them there. Take the time to hold up every new teaching in the light of scripture. That is discernment, because when we know the truth, the lies become obvious.

Marvin Rosenthal, founder of *Zion's Hope* has said, *"Human history is moving toward 17 acres,"*[6] meaning, Mt. Moriah, the temple mount where God's dwelling on earth was located.

Israel, I'm sure, is weary of the constant war that's gone on since 1948 and would welcome a treaty or covenant that would protect them from Arab and Muslim nations. In fact, all would welcome a new world order that would bring peace to this area, even to the point of allowing for a temple to be rebuilt to keep that peace.

Scripture says for 42 months there will be peace. Then the *abomination that causes desolation* appears. The antichrist performs the ultimate sacrilege; he blasphemes God and all holiness, having an image of himself placed in the rebuilt temple.

The lie is displayed graphically; man is god. But the antichrist does not do this alone. A world religious leader makes it happen, drawing the world to the antichrist's feet. This second beast is the ultimate false prophet. As religious belief intensifies worldwide, satan is putting in place counterfeit *religious attitudes* necessary for people to believe his lie.[7]

Can you see how this can come together now?

False prophets always have a false messiah - that is "man." Man is at the center, not God. That's the mark of a cult. The New Age teaching today is that we are all gods, and we need to discover our divinity from earth, or some cosmic experience, or eastern meditation, etc. Feelings become more important than truth. .

Here's the truth: God alone is the Creator. We are His creation, we are His creatures, and we are His children. He is worthy of all praise and He should be worshiped because of it!

There is a spirit of humanism that is prevalent today. It leaves God out and man becomes the hero. With these growing cults, man fills the void in man, not God. When you're listening to what is being said, either at church, TV, radio, books, movies or podcasts - listen to see who is at the center of the message. If it's not pointing you to Jesus, then it is a false message with man at the center. Matthew 7:15 says:

> *"Beware of the false prophets, who come to you in sheep's clothing, but inwardly are ravenous wolves."*

The Image

In 13:14-15, John tells us there was an image built and the wounded beast:

> *"...was given power to give breath to the image of the first beast,*

so that it could speak and cause all who refused to worship the image to be killed."

This image that can breathe and speak has a kind of special effects quality that seems to suggest state-of-the-art technology more than the true ability to grant life. God Almighty alone is the life-giver.

Remember, satan's kingdom is built on cruel force and deception. There is no love, compassion or mercy. Just hate towards God and anyone who loves Him.

The Mark of the Beast

There will come a time during this period of forced worship when the *mark of the beast* will be prevalent. John says the beast has a number and it is 666. Having it will be necessary for the economy because we will all live in a cashless culture by then. We are almost there now:

> *"And he causes all, the small and the great, and the rich and the poor, and the free men and the slaves, to be given a mark on their right hand or on their forehead, and he provides that no one will be able to buy or to sell, except the one who has the mark, either the name of the beast or the number of his name."*
>
> Revelation 13:16-17

That is a counterfeit, an imitation of God. God has marked all believers with a seal of the Holy Spirit.

> *"And you also were included in Christ when you heard the message of truth, the gospel of your salvation. When you believed, you were marked in Him with a seal, the promised Holy Spirit, who is a deposit guaranteeing our inheritance until the redemption of those who are God's possession - to the praise of his glory."*
>
> Ephesians 1:13-14

We must remember that we were bought with Christ's blood. We are His. But this world is not our home. Do not hold on to your material possessions so hard. This will be a very dark and serious time for all who follow Christ. Your car, home, your 401K's will not save you or keep you from the evil that will come through this tribulation time. The only solid guarantee is knowing, trusting and following Jesus Christ. Period. Be prepared.

Many ask, 'will the church be present during these end times?'

- Many Bible interpreters feel Scripture teaches that we will be spared its horrors. They contend that the rapture of the church will occur before this devastating time.
- Others who are just as sincere, are convinced that the true church, the bride of Christ, will still be here and will suffer at the hands of the antichrist.

None of us really know for sure. Scripture is left up to interpretation here. We can't all be right, but we can all be ready. Here's a few reminders that can help you to get ready:

- Do not believe that just because people do miracles that they are from God.
- Ask the Holy Spirit for discernment.
- Check all teachings through scripture and make sure the content is right.
- Don't get caught up in the speculations of the end times. Trust that this is all under God's control, and we are already marked with His mark and saved for eternity.
- This is not our home.
- Conquer the devil by the blood of the Lamb and the Word of your testimony.

> *"The devil wrestles with God, and the field of battle is the human heart."*
>
> Fyodor Dostoyevsky

Endnotes:

1. Community Bible Study TD Helps; 2008; Lesson 16; pg 41
2. Community Bible Study Revelation Commentary by Timothy Crater, 1997-2004, Lesson 16, pg 1
3. Ibid., pg 2
4. Kendall Easely, Revelation- Holman New Testament Commentary 1998 B & H Publishing Group; Nashville,TN; pg 227
5. Community Bible Study TD Helps; 2008; Lesson 16; pg 43
6. http://www.zionshope.org/index_fix.aspx
7. Community Bible Study TD Helps; 2008; Lesson 17; pg 45

Chapter 14

Thi chapter opens with Jesus standing on Mt. Zion, with 144,000 believers. Commentators question whether this takes place in heaven or on earth. Many believe it is heaven. Mt. Zion was a standard first century Christian name for heaven.

> *"But you have come to Mount Zion, to the heavenly Jerusalem, the city of the living God. You have come to thousands upon thousands of angels in joyful assembly."*

Hebrews 12:22

The throne is there, along with four living creatures and the 24 elders.

The 144,000

Who are the 144,000? They could be the same as those mentioned in Revelation 7:4:

> *"Then I heard the number of those who were sealed: 144,000 from all the tribes of Israel."*

This is believed to be the sealed Jewish believers who come out of the Tribulation. The ones protected from God's wrath. This is a picture of the future; Jesus reigns on Zion with those who belong to Him.

Commentator Phyllis Cooper brings some clarity to us in regards to this 144.000:

> *"What does it mean to be "sealed" by God? In Chapter Seven, an angel gave instruction that no harm could come to the earth until the 144,000 had been sealed. God intended to protect His chosen people from His wrath, which was about to be poured out.*

"In 14:1, we see the Lamb (our King) and the 144,000 standing together on the mount.

"Were these 144,000 martyred? Interpreters have differing opinions. If we consider the possibility that the 144,000 remain alive on earth throughout the day the Lord, and then join the heavenly harpists in praise, we see an encouraging picture of the harmony between heaven and earth during Christ's kingdom. But that is not the crucial issue. God "sealed" these people not just for a few years but for eternity. Not one of the 144,000 is lost. When the Bible says to us, "Having believed, you were marked in Him with a seal, the promised Holy Spirit, who is a deposit guaranteeing our inheritance until the redemption of those who are God's possession—to the praise of His glory." (Ephesians 1:13b-14), we can depend on it. So take heart, God won't lose us either."[4]

Our daughter was called by the Lord to travel on a six-month mission's trip to Australia, Korea and Malaysia when she was only 18 years old. The longest she had ever been away from home was just under two weeks, and that was a trip made with her youth group at church. She was with all her friends and she was, for the most part, safe. My little girl was traveling far away from her home, by herself. Thoughts and fears would overwhelm me at times. *What was I doing allowing this? She's so young. Will she be alright? Will she be safe? I can't be there if she needs me.*

As I cried out in prayer, the Lord reminded me that she is a sealed believer in Jesus. Regardless of what happens, she is His and belongs to Him. She is my child, but she is God's gift to me. She is really *His*. Knowing this made it is easier to let her go, because by God's grace she is secure.

We must remember that our Father in Heaven loves each and every one of us even more than we love our own children. He proved that love through the cross. Those who by faith are His children are sealed.

You are secure. Nothing in this life, not the devil, the antichrist, the false prophet or even death will ever snatch you out of His hands.

Jesus Wants Everyone To Believe

In 11:6 our focus shifts back to Earth - to those who remain, the unfaithful.

At this point, half the population has already been wiped out in the seal-

and-trumpet judgments. The antichrist and false prophet have killed most of the believers who refuse the mark of the beast. With most of the Lord's faithful witnesses gone, God still won't give up on non-believers until the final judgment. He sends an angel and He calls in the hosts of heaven to proclaim His Gospel. This is the only hope of salvation to all who remain - every nation, tribe, language and people. (14:6-7)

Here may be mankind's last chance to respond to the good news of salvation. Jesus says:

> *"This gospel of the kingdom will be preached in the whole world as a testimony to all nations, and then the end will come."*
>
> Matthew 24:14

Our God is relentless. He is the Hound of Heaven. Many are fleeing from their only hope for eternity. He is the true Shepherd and wishes for all His sheep to be with Him. Isn't it comforting to know that as long as they can draw a breath, God will not relent? That's how big His love is.

Through the message of the third angel in 14:9, God makes clear the horror of the end for all who choose the beast over the Lamb. Some people recoil at this, saying a God of love could never allow people to suffer eternal torment. We must remember that God's love is a *holy love*, not based on feelings. He sent His Son as the perfect sacrifice so that all who trust in Him would never have to suffer in hell.

Jesus shed His blood on the cross, enduring the sinner's destiny of separation from God - spiritual death - so that we could live eternally.[2] That is what our great God of love, did for us.

We all have a choice to believe Jesus or not. But God is showing us after revealing the glory of heaven and the hope of the earth, the somber picture of the reality of hell. This is what's in store for those who choose to turn from God and receive the mark of the beast, and worship his image (14:9):

- They will taste the full strength of fury of God's wrath. (14:10)
- They will be tormented with burning sulfur. (14:10)
- The smoke of their torment will rise forever. (14:11)
- There will be no rest day or night. (14:11)[3]

A lot of jokes are made about hell. But the hell revealed to us in verses

8-13 is no laughing matter. Hell is eternal torment, day and night, unrelenting torment. A righteous God cannot co-exist with unrighteousness. God doesn't send people to hell; they do that on their own by their own choices.

There aren't many sure bets in this life, except death and taxes. Others decide for us when and how much tax we will pay. But how we experience death is directly controlled by our own personal choice in this life. Jesus is the only sure bet for eternity.

Jesus Christ died because God didn't want His children to perish. He sacrificed His Son for us. If you do not know, or if you are not sure you know Jesus Christ, stop reading and ask Jesus into your heart at this very moment. Do it now while there is still time. Proclaim that He is the Son of God and that you want Him to live in you. There is a time when heaven will shut its doors and there will be no way to spend eternity with Him. Separation from God *is Hell.*

Say this prayer out loud with me:

> *Heavenly Father, I am a sinner and I am lost. Thank You for forgiving me of my sins. I know in my heart that Jesus Christ is Your Son and that He came to die for me, so that I might live with You in eternity. With that knowledge, I am asking Jesus to come and live in my heart right now. I invite the Holy Spirit to dwell in me as well. I love you Father and thank you for loving me so much. In Jesus' Name, Amen.*

It's that simple. It is not complicated. You made a choice, the right choice. You are His and He is yours. May you feel His love for you dwell inside of you every day until the day that you part from this earth.

The Harvest of the Earth

As we continue with chapter 14, John's vision in 14:14, begins with Jesus, the Son of Man, sitting on a cloud, with a sickle in His hand. The time has finally arrived. The long awaited harvest is here.

In 14:14-16 it speaks of reaping, like that of wheat (Jesus reaps, gathering in the harvest of the righteous believers). In 14:17-20 it speaks of a harvest, like that of grapes (an angel of fire gathers the unbelievers and throws them into the winepress of God's wrath). They are trampled, and their blood creates a 1,600 stadia (a 180 mile) river as high as a horse's bridle.

To drive from Nashville, Tennessee to Louisville, Kentucky is 175.5

miles. It takes two hours and 45 minutes to get there by car according to Mapquest.com. Now imagine a river of blood that comes up to a horse's bridle (which is near, the top of the neck). That is the length from Nashville to Louisville. That's even five miles short of what scripture says.

Depending on how you interpret scripture, this could be a figurative or a literal statement. Either way, there is a lot of bloodshed!

Julia Ward Howe was perhaps the most famous American woman of the nineteenth century. Her beloved song, *"The Battle Hymn of the Republic,"* was a result of her visiting Union military camps near Washington, DC in 1861. She saw the events of her day a fulfillment of the gruesome prophecy of a horrible bloodbath between the forces of righteousness and the powers of darkness. Read these lyrics with this chapter in mind.

> *"Mine eyes have seen the glory of the coming of the Lord;*
> *He is trampling out the vintage*
> *where the grapes of wrath are stored;*
> *He hath loosed the fateful lighting of His terrible swift sword;*
> *His truth is marching on.*
> *Glory, glory halleluiah. Glory, glory halleluiah.*
> *Glory, glory halleluiah. Our God is marching on."*[4]

While the Civil War may have been a preliminary shadow of what John foresaw in Revelation 14, by no means did it fulfill the prophecy. And the events of our day may also be preliminary fulfillments of prophecy. But one day, we will know for sure that the final day, the final battle will come. This coming day will be a day of truth. It will be a perfect judgment by a righteous God.

The final harvest will be a great and terrible *day*. It is not an abstract, symbolic, theological concept. Jesus was born on a *day*.

- He died on a *day*.
- He was resurrected on a *day*.
- And He will come again and He will judge on that *day*.

Stay focused on the bigger picture.

> *"But in keeping with His promise we are looking forward to a new*
> *heaven and a new earth, the home of righteousness. So then, dear*
> *friends, since you are looking forward to this, make every effort to*
> *be found spotless, blameless and at peace with Him."*
>
> 2 Peter 3:13-14

Endnotes:

1. Community Bible Study Revelation Commentary by Phyllis Cooper, 1997-2004, Lesson 18, pg 2
2. Community Bible Study TD Helps; 2008; Lesson 18; pg 48
3. Ibid., pg.49
4. "Battle Hymn of the Republic" Lyrics by Julia Ward Howe (1819-1910), Public Domain

CHAPTER 15

Back in chapter 8, we saw how the breaking of the seventh seal allowed the scroll to unroll and the seven trumpet judgments to begin. Here in chapter 15, we see the prelude to the seven bowl judgments, which are the judgments of the seventh trumpet.

The seven final bowls of God's wrath must be poured out on earth prior to the Second Coming of Christ. John sees:

> *"...those who had been victorious over the beast and his image and over the number of his name."*

Revelation 15:2

These saints have overcome. They overcame the beast, the antichrist, by not buckling in to political pressure to reject Christ. They overcame the false prophet and the religious pressure to reject Christ. They overcame the economic pressure to receive the mark of the beast,[1] and now they stand in heaven as victors. They have beaten the beast and live in triumph. They are being honored in glory before God's very throne.

Some of these saints overcame by becoming martyrs (where the antichrist conquered or "overcame" the saints in 13:7), but nothing indicates that the overcomers are restricted to the martyrs.

They sing a song with two titles: "The Song of Moses" and "The Song of the Lamb." They are holding harps that were given to them by God (15:2). What an honor to sing a heavenly song of victory. It reflects and resembles a song of triumph and of redemption. It was sung by the Israelites and Moses after they were set free from captivity and left Egypt, knowing all of it happened by God's hand. The "Song of Moses" is found in Exodus 15:1-18. During this time, Moses was being used by God to voice the warnings and bring about the plagues. In the New Testament that same voice would be Jesus Christ. Pharaoh is similar to the beast with its wickedness. The Israelites' escape from bondage into the Promised Land is similar to our escaping the beast's bondage and coming into eternity. The song has two titles because one is of an Old Testament victory, and the other is similar, but it is sung unto the Lamb of God.[2]

There are preparations being completed in the heavenly temple. The four living creatures give golden bowls to seven angels. These bowls are vessels from which God's wrath is to be poured upon the earth. Seven angels are dressed in *"clean shining linen and wore golden sashes around their chests."* (15:6) They come out from the Most Holy Place where God dwells. The smoke from God's Holy glory seems overwhelming. But the most sobering fact of all is that *"no one could enter the temple."* (15:8) Why?

- God is absolutely holy.
- He is higher than we are.
- He is perfect and pure.
- He is called the Holy One of Israel.
- His Spirit is called the Holy Spirit.

In Isaiah 6:3, we see the sovereignty of God's holiness as the angels worship Him and cry:

> *"Holy, holy, holy is the Lord Almighty; the whole earth is full of His glory."*

God is to be revered, on earth and in heaven. When humans trample on God's holiness by their sinfulness, God demonstrates His wrath against sin through judgment. If we have been wronged, we need to trust Him with the final word and not take it upon ourselves. In justice and righteousness, God shows Himself always as sovereign and holy.[3]

Those who respond to God's offer of mercy, by trusting and submitting to Him as Lord, are covered by Christ's righteousness. Those who reject Christ as Lord, come under God's wrath and they will be judged for their sins. God carefully measures out His wrath with seven last bowl judgments.

God's mercy is still available to us. But one day God's patience will be over. His wrath against sin will flow. The door to the temple will be shut. Where are you in this story?

The decision is yours.

Endnotes:

1. Kendall Easely, Revelation- Holman New Testament Commentary 1998 B & H Publishing Group; Nashville,TN; pg 271
2. Community Bible Study Revelation Commentary by Timothy Crater, 1997-2004, Lesson 19, pg 5
3. Community Bible Study Revelation Commentary by Phyllis Cooper, 1997-2004, Lesson 19, pg 8

CHAPTER 16

There's an ancient fable told about a greedy king named Midas. He wished that everything he touched would turn to gold. His wish was granted. At first it was great, but then the problems began. His food, his water and even the people he loved the most turned to gold. Eventually, King Midas's desire became his downfall. He had all the gold in the world, but died alone and broken.

The moral of the story? Be careful what you wish for.

In this chapter, satan and his unbelieving world will reap God's wrath in the final harvest.[1]

The Seven Bowl Judgments of God's Wrath

These seven bowl judgments are far more severe than the trumpet judgments of chapter 8, although these bowl judgments offer certain similarities with what the Lord sent to Pharaoh as well. Compare the seven bowl judgments with the seven plagues as they complete God's judgment on this rebellious world.

Bowl #1

16:2 *"The first angel went and poured out his bowl on the land and ugly and painful sores broke out on the people who had the mark of the beast and worshiped his image."* (This is much like the painful sores of the sixth plague on the Egyptians from Exodus 9.)

It's as if God were saying to the worshipers of the antichrist: "You like the marks of evil on your body? You want to force My people to bear the mark of this wicked one? Then you will bear the painul mark of My judgment for it."[2]

Bowl #2

16:3 *"The second angel poured out his bowl on the sea, and it turned into blood like that of a dead man, and every living thing in the sea died."* This is what happened to the rivers with Moses and Pharaoh. (Exodus 7) In the trumpet judgment (chapter 8), only one-third of the living things in the oceans die, but here *every* living thing in the sea dies.

Once more, God returns upon the wicked a judgment that corresponds to their evil. The wicked have shed the blood of the righteous, including the 144,000 and the victorious saints we read about at the beginning of chapter 15. Those who have shown such a fondness for shedding blood can now fill the oceans with theirs. And that is only the beginning.[3]

Bowl #3

16:4 *"The third angel poured out his bowl on the rivers and springs of water, and they became blood."*

This judgment is on the drinkable water, which is more necessary to sustain life. Now *all* water is affected; the sea, oceans, rivers and lakes. The fishing industry, which supplies much of the food around the world, is ruined. Fresh water is no longer fit for drinking. Will water filtration systems be able to cope? Commerce will come to a standstill as people search for that one element that is essential to life - water. And can you imagine the smell of rotting fish from the oceans, seas and rivers?[4]

Bowl #4

16:8 *"The forth angel poured out his bowl on the sun, and the sun was given power to scorch people with fire. They were seared by the intense heat and they cursed the name of God..."*

God turns up the furnace from the sun so that people are seared with intense heat. This too is a fitting judgment, for these wicked people had turned up the heat of persecution and affliction of God's people. It's amazing to still see that the wicked harden their heart and won't repent. Just like Pharaoh's heart in Exodus 8. They will not glorify God, so God will show them no mercy.[5]

Bowl #5

16:10 *"The fifth angel poured out his bowl on the throne of the beast, and his kingdom was plunged into darkness."* This bowl judgment shows God is becoming more specific and precise in His wrath. He focuses on the throne of the beast. In the fifth trumpet, the sun and sky were also darkened, as was Egypt under one of the plagues (Exodus 10).

Commentator Timothy Crater clarifies this for us:

> *"The kingdom of the antichrist alone is plunged into darkness. This may mean that his original national jurisdiction, the three nations that he plucks up and makes his own, as well as the other seven that are part of his coalition, are all turned dark.*
>
> *Like the other judgments, this one too fits the crime. Those who have loved darkness rather than light now get more of it than they bargained for. And they are terrified. They had extinguished God's human lights by martyrdom, and God turns off their lights in response. This darkness is not a pleasant experience for them because scripture says, "men gnawed their tongues in agony." (16:10) They blame God for all their problems and issues. They never blame themselves.*
>
> *So their external darkness exactly parallels the deep remorselessness of their souls."*[6]

I remember years ago, we took a trip to Mammoth Caves in Kentucky with the kids. The guide took 15 to 20 of us way down deep underground on this tour. When we got to as far as the tour would take us, they told us to not move, to turn our flash lights off and to wait until they heard us say to turn them on again. When we did, it was black. At first, I waited for my eyes to adjust to the darkness, but they never did. There was not light for them to adjust to, because it was truly pitch black. I kept waving my hand in front of my face but I couldn't see it. I could feel the breeze my waving hand caused, but I simply could not see it. The guides waited until they could sense the anxiety in the room rise. They knew none of us had experienced total darkness like this before. It's very un-nerving. The unsettling darkness, the feeling of separation and isolation that experience brings, is just a taste of what is in store for these unbelievers. It is total and complete darkness with no light... and no hope.

Bowl #6

16:12 *"The sixth angel poured out his bowl on the great river Euphrates, its water was dried up to prepare the way for the kings from the East."*

This passage makes it clear that the kings of the earth and their armies are being divinely gathered to Armageddon for a great battle. The Euphrates is the eastern boundary of the land God gave to Abraham and his children. The river forms a natural barrier to any major movements westward into the land of Israel.

These kings will come from the East, so they could be of Arab or Asian descent.

In addition to what is happening on the Euphrates, John also sees three evil spirits that look like frogs (16:3), corresponding to the second plague in Egypt (Exodus 8). The repulsive nature of the frogs is just like the demons they represent and is consistent with them coming from the same river as the four fallen spirits we learned about from the sixth trumpet judgment. These frogs come out of the mouths of the dragon, the beast and the false prophet. They speak lies and perform miraculous signs.[7]

Let's think about lies for a moment. Lies are ugly, filthy, devious things. In this case they are even more insidious because they are dripping in beautiful words that deceive the masses. These lies are probably "religious terms" and the "frogs" convince the nations of the world to come to battle. As with all such deceptions, the nations believe they will be battling each other, but satan's agenda is a final clash between his evil forces and God for the ownership of the earth and headship over creation.

That's how it is with lies; liars themselves are deceived, thinking they are doing themselves a favor, when actually they are pawns in the hand of satan.[8]

Jesus Christ is the truth. His Word is truth. We, as Christians, are to know the truth and to stand for it. Anything less is playing with, well, frogs.

It seems ridiculous to think that anyone would deliberately choose to go to war against Almighty God. But if you think about it, we do it every day. We fight for control, for dominion over our lives. (i.e. finances, work, relationships, etc.). By refusing to give God dominion over what already belongs to Him, we put ourselves at war with Him. Ultimately, we stand against Him.[9] Sounds harsh, I know, but that's the truth.

If there are areas in you that you know need changing, don't panic, but pray. Ask God to help your desires conform to His desires. He knows what's best for you. He loves you. Just release it and surrender it to Him. After all, Psalm 37:4 says:

> *"Take delight in the LORD, and He will give you the desires of your heart."*

Verse 15 says that the Lord will come like a thief. We must stay spiritually awake and alert for His coming. How do we do this? By knowing and studying His Word. To know His truth.

Paul helps us by describing the kind of lives we are to lead as we wait for the day of the Lord:

> *"We do not belong to the night or the darkness…But since we belong to the day, let us be self-controlled, putting on faith and love as a breastplate, and the hope of salvation as a helmet."*
>
> 1 Thessalonians 5:5-8

This should be part of our daily routine when getting dressed for the day. If we practice this, we will be both blessed and ready to meet Jesus.

Verse 16 says the kings gather to the place that in Hebrew is called Armageddon. This name occurs only once in the Bible and it is designating the place where the last great battle of the ages will take place (Revelation 16:16). It will coincide with the second coming of Christ (Revelation 16:15) and there all of the hosts of evil will be defeated. (Revelation 19:11-21). Even though Armageddon is a Hebrew word, it does not occur in the Old Testament. Its meaning is not exactly clear, but it is best taken to mean Mount Megiddo, since "Har" in Hebrew means mountain and "Mageddon" is the place-name of Megiddo. There is no Hebrew reference for a Har-Megiddo. In Old Testament history, there was a city named Megiddo. It was located in a strategic geographic pass in Israel. It sat on a hill 70 feet above the valley of Jezreel, which extended all the way to Mount Tabor. It was a place of numerous decisive battles that were fought because of the broad plain that stood before it.[10]

1. Deborah and Barak defeated Sisera and his Canaanite army there (Judges 4-5).
2. Gideon drove off the Midianites and Amalekites there (Judges 6).
3. Saul and the army of Israel were defeated because of their failure to trust in God there (1 Samuel 31).

4. The Egyptian army under Pharaoh Neco killed Josiah, king of Judah there (2 Kings 23:29).

This location is likely the site of the world's last and final battle. A battle that Christ Himself will be present at. We'll read about this in chapter 19.

Bowl #7

16:17-20 *"The seventh angel poured out his bowl into the air, and out of the temple came a loud voice from the throne saying, "It is done." Then there came flashes of lighting, rumblings, peals of thunder and a severe earthquake. No earthquake like it has ever occurred since man has been on earth, so tremendous was the quake."*

In both the seventh trumpet judgment and the seventh bowl judgment, there are temple displays of lightning, thunder, hailstones, heavenly voices and earthquakes.

What makes this last bowl judgment unique?

It is poured into the air. It's an atmosphere that surrounds all the earth. The announcement from the temple that *"It is done,"* suggests that this judgment finishes God's wrath - collapsing the world system and opening the way for the kingdom of God.

Jesus Christ saying *"It is finished"* when on the cross, and God saying *"It is done"* in this passage, should encourage us that there is a deliberate plan in place, a bigger picture than we can comprehend, and that God is in complete control of it.

In verse 19 we see the collapse of Babylon the Great and the cities of the nations. This is likely a spiritual name given to a "great city" of the last days. This city will be:

- A great port city and commercial power.
- A place of vicious persecution of believers in Jesus Christ.
- An evil counterfeit of the holy city - the true Jerusalem, just like the antichrist is a counterfeit of Christ Himself.

Verse 19 also says it will be *"split into three parts"* by the seventh bowl judgment, and its daughter cities among the nations will likewise collapse as God gives her (and them) the full *"fury of His wrath."* (We will discuss the fall of Babylon in the next chapter.)

This earthquake is an upheaval of islands, mountains and possibly even continents, and they are all radically moved. The entire topography of the earth changes. In 16:21 there will be hundred-pound hailstones that fall upon the earth. This seems like a kind of divine stoning from their Creator. Some will still curse God instead of turning from their wicked ways. They are stiff-necked and unrepentant to their bitter and defiant end.[11]

The Trumpets and Bowls

The trumpets picture judgments in their early stages, while the bowls reveal their ultimate fulfillment in all their intensity. The time sequence for the bowl judgments suggests that they may occur over days, instead of months or years.

One thing is for sure - God's wrath is vast and thorough. Another thing that is certain - God's promises are true. He promises to punish the wicked, so we don't need to attempt to "get even" with people for any real or perceived wrongs, because God will handle vengeance. Paul reminds us in Romans:

> *"Beloved, never avenge yourselves, but leave it to the wrath of God,*
> *for it is written, 'Vengeance is Mine, I will repay, says the Lord.'"*
>
> Romans 12:19 (ESV)

Endnotes:

1. Community Bible Study TD Helps; 2009; Lesson 20; pg 54
2. Community Bible Study Revelation Commentary by Timothy Crater, 1997-2004, Lesson 20, pg 1
3. Ibid., pg 2
4. Ibid., pg 2-3
5. Ibid., pg 3-4
6. Ibid., pg 4
7. Ibid., pg 4-5
8. Community Bible Study Revelation Commentary by Phyllis Cooper, 1997-2004, Lesson 20, pg 5
9. Community Bible Study TD Helps; 2009; Lesson 20; pg 55
10. Kendall Easely, Revelation- Holman New Testament Commentary 1998 B & H Publishing Group; Nashville,TN; pg 290
11. Community Bible Study Revelation Commentary by Timothy Crater, 1997-2004, Lesson 20, pg 6-7

CHAPTER 17

"This city [of mankind] is earthly both in its beginning and in its end—a city in which nothing more is hoped for than can be seen in this world."

St. Augustine of Hippo
"The City of God"

For 1,000 yrs., the Christian thinker with the greatest influence was St. Augustine of Hippo. His longest book, "The City of God," interpreted history as the story of two cities - the struggle between those who depend on God and those who rely on themselves.

One city that is focused on is Babel, which was located on the plain of Shinar, Babylonia - today known as northeastern Syria. Genesis 11:1-9 records man's rebellious attempts to build a tower to heaven, a tremendous human project, to celebrate man's proud dominion of the earth. The focus was on man and not God. Its builders reasoned:

"Let us build ourselves a city, with a tower that reaches to the heavens, so that we may make a name for ourselves and not be scattered over the face of the whole earth."

Genesis 11:4

In the case of Babel, God directly intervened, but He has not stopped humans from applying these same principles to their other cities and civilizations. The ruins of countless other ancient cities confirm their parallels with Babel.

Babel was the model. Consider these other ancient cities and their civilizations:

- Memphis of the Egyptian Kingdom
- Nineveh of the Assyrian Empire

- Babylon of the New Babylonian Empire
- Persepolis of the Persian Empire
- Antioch of the Seleucid Empire
- Rome of the Roman Republic and Empire

Each was the Babel of its Own Day

1. Each rose to an expression of engineering ingenuity, supported by military force and political scheming.
2. Each was a commercial, religious and cultural center.
3. Each proudly opposed God and the people of God.

Roll them all together and they become the perfect forerunner for one future final great city and civilization opposed to God - referred by John as Babylon the Great. As with that first great city, so it will be with the last great city. God will judge her directly and dramatically.[1]

Chapter 17 opens with an angel promising to show John *"the punishment of the great prostitute."* (17:1) Then 17:2 reveals the angel giving John an explanation of the prostitute's sins, stating that both kings and the common people had defiled themselves with her. They violated standards of righteousness and justice to gain her favors. In fact, the whole earth embraces the decadence, idolatry and corruption of Babylon the Great.

Keeping in mind that John, in 11:8 has already explained that Jerusalem is figuratively called *Sodom* and *Egypt*, it is possible that Babylon is also a figurative name for a tribulation capital of corruption.[2] This city's influence is clearly felt worldwide.

The Beast and The Woman

In 17:3, the scene of the vision is a desolate, lifeless wilderness. This could be the reflection of the barren spiritual nature of the woman he is about to describe.

John Describes The Beast

1. The beast is scarlet - perhaps it represents royalty. As we've seen, both its seven heads and ten horns represent kings. In the ancient world, scarlet represented royal opulence. But this color may also be connected to what Isaiah said in 1:18, *"...though your sins are like scarlet."* (Maybe this is why in most cities the darkest

areas, spiritually speaking, are known as the "red light" district).

2. The beast is covered with blasphemous names, perhaps signifying not only evil slanders against God, but also its outrageous claims of deity. This is similar to what we saw with the antichrist and his blasphemy in chapter 13.

3. With the mention of the seven heads and ten horns we know these are not only kings, but they are under the same political alliance. The beast represents the political alliance of the last days, and the woman is a city Babylon the Great - which in some crucial sense rides upon, or controls this great beastly alliance…for a time.[3]

John Describes The Woman

1. Her dress is scarlet overlaid with purple in their intensity (a contrast to the spotless white linen of the saints, who are the bride of the Lamb).

2. John notes her accessories. This is the garb of a great prostitute. The sinful city is loaded down with material opulence and moral decadence.

3. Her golden cup carries *"abominable things and the filth of her adulteries."* (17:4)

4. Written on her forehead is: *"MYSTERY; BABYLON THE GREAT; THE MOTHER OF PROSTITUTES; AND THE ABOMINATIONS OF THE EARTH."* The word, mystery, is one of the names she wears on her forehead. In those days, Roman prostitutes would wear the names of their owners or pimps on their foreheads. In 2 Thessalonians 2:6-8 it says:

   "And you know what restrains him now, so that in his time he will be revealed. For the mystery of lawlessness is already at work; only He who now restrains will do so until he is taken out of the way. Then that lawless one will be revealed whom the Lord will slay with the breath of His mouth and bring to an end by the appearance of his coming…"

   God is in control and only He knows what satan is capable of if his fury is unleashed. *We don't.* It's a mystery to us right now and satan is still having to abide in the boundaries that God has set for him. The rest of the names are, well, self explanatory.

5. Her intoxication of the blood of the saints, who bore the testimony of Jesus Christ, will flow freely in the streets.

Just as ancient Babylon had murdered the Old Testament people of God along with destroying Jerusalem and taking some survivors into captivity in 586 B.C. (just look in 2 Kings 25), so this new Babylon will murder the people of God too. This description would have made the first century Christians think of Rome and its official persecutions under Nero and Domitian. They were brutal in their killing of Christians. And yet, that will pale in comparison with what will come.[4]

Here's a mind-blowing statistic; more Christians were martyred in the twentieth century than in the previous nineteen *combined*.[5] Wow! Things appear to be heating up.

John is astonished at this vision of the woman and the beast she rides in 17:7-8.

The *"once was, now is not, and will come"* in 17:8 has posed some difficulty to interpreters. Here's a few examples of what I've found that offer some possible explanations;

- If looking at this historically, the phrase suggests that the beast existed at an earlier time in history (or was present). Yet at the time John received his Revelation, the beast did not exist, but would appear on the earth again during the Tribulation. It's quite possible this could be the demon-like king that was over the scorpion locusts in 9:11 and would reappear when the Abyss was opened.
- If looking at this personally, the *"was, is not, will come"* phrase, could refer to the mortal head wound on the beast that the antichrist will suffer; meaning he lived, died, and rose back to life.
- Still others believe the reappearance of the beast in this same verse refers to his satanic world government once again coming to power as a revived empire. Confusion comes because satan, the antichrist, and his world government are all so closely related.[6]

Regardless, this is yet again his attempt to counterfeit and imitate Christ:

> *"...the One who is, and who was, and who is to come."*

> Revelation 1:8

The angel observes the public response to the beast in 17:8. The ones whose *"names have not been written in the book of life from the creation of the world"* 17:8 (the ones who do not believe in Christ), will be captivated, seduced and enthralled by this beast. Paul mentions this to the Thessalonians.

> *"The coming of the lawless one will be in accordance with how satan works. He will use all sorts of displays of power through signs and wonders that serve the lie, and all the ways that wickedness deceives those who are perishing. They perish because they refused to love the truth and so be saved. For this reason God sends them a powerful delusion so that they will believe the lie and so that all will be condemned who have not believed the truth but have delighted in wickedness."*

> 2 Thessalonians 2:9-12

I think that is the sweet and sour part of scripture the angel told John about, which he also ate. (10:9) The angel then says that *"this calls for a mind with wisdom."* This tells us that these next verses ahead will be interpretive curves and twists, so hang on.

The Seven Hills

Hills may be another way of referring to historic kingdoms or empires. In 17:10, the angel indicates that five of the heads/hills/kings fell in John's time, one currently existed and another was yet to come.

The five fallen kingdoms were military powers, and all opposed God's people. You may recall me mentioning the prostitute city in the last chapter. Let's take a look at some other prostitute cities from the past:

1. Egypt - during the days of the Israelite slavery tried to destroy the chosen people by ordering all male babies killed. (Exodus 1) The prostitute city at that time, in 16th century B.C., was Memphis.
2. Assyria - during the days of the prophets Hosea and Isaiah destroyed the ten northern tribes of Israel in 722 B.C. (2 Kings 15). The prostitute city of that time was Nineveh, the original great city of the Old Testament (see the Book of Jonah).
3. Babylonia - during the days of Jeremiah and Ezekiel, Nebuchadnezzar destroyed and burned Jerusalem and took the tribes of Judah into captivity in 586 B.C. (2 Kings 25). The prostitute city was Babylon on the Euphrates.
4. Persia - during the days of Queen Esther (about 460 B.C.), came close to destroying every Jew because of the plotting of Haman.

Modern Jews still remember this event with the annual Feast of Purim. The prostitute city was Persepolis.

5. The Seleucid Empire - was a successor to part of Alexander the Great's realm. Under Antiochus IV Epiphanes (known as the "abomination that causes desolation," because he profaned the temple altar), in 168 B.C., destroys the temple of Jerusalem and outlawed the practice of Judaism. The prostitute city was Antioch.[7]

These then would be the five fallen kingdoms.

Historians point to the city of Rome as the sixth city, which persecuted the Jews. Titus completely destroyed the temple in Jerusalem in 70 A.D. This sixth kingdom, which existed in John's time is likely the Roman Empire. The seventh *"has yet to come,"* and the antichrist will be the eighth king according to 17:11.

Then who is the seventh king? The one who was future to John and yet one who *"must remain for a little while."* (17:10)

Some interpreters point to a twentieth century man who persecuted and killed millions of Jews during WWII. Yet he only remained for a brief time. We know him as Adolf Hitler. But one can only guess.

We do know however that the beast will lead the 8th kingdom, and the ten horns are the ten simultaneous rulers in the alliance that supports this future world leader. The ten/seven political alliance, or the configuration of it is found in the book of Daniel 7:7-8. As I mentioned earlier, the alliance starts with the ten kings but resolves to seven when the antichrist emerges, takes over one of the ten and will incorporate three of the others into this rule - leaving a total of seven kings.[8]

There will be a rallying cry for unity with a one world government which results in a one world empire. There have been calls for a one world government for a long time. Some say it will bring peace to every country. They cite how much easier it will be to travel with no borders and no need to change money, etc.

But they don't mention such unity will include a unified world religion too, and it certainly will not be Christianity. The beast who will rule in the eighth kingdom will clearly persecute God's people: both Christian and Jew.

The beast's ten horns or kings will come to hate the woman (Babylon) and turn on her and destroy her. God will turn the wicked on themselves to accomplish His purpose and their end. I know it seems crazy, but God has all of this under His control. He is sovereign and just and His ways are not ours. As we stay alert to His Word, I am sure we may be given the eyes to recognize this city. Take 1 Timothy 4:16 to heart:

> *"Watch your life and doctrine closely. Persevere in them, because if you do, you will save both yourself and your hearers."*

Endnotes:

1. Kendall Easely, Revelation- Holman New Testament Commentary 1998 B & H Publishing Group; Nashville,TN; pg 303
2. Community Bible Study Revelation Commentary by Timothy Crater, 1997-2004, Lesson 21, pg 1
3. Ibid., pg 2
4. Kendall Easely, Revelation- Holman New Testament Commentary 1998 B & H Publishing Group; Nashville,TN; pg 305,307
5. Community Bible Study Revelation Commentary by Phyllis Cooper 1997-2004, Lesson 21, pg 4
6. Community Bible Study Revelation Commentary by Timothy Crater, 1997-2004, Lesson 21, pg 4-5
7. Kendall Easely, Revelation- Holman New Testament Commentary 1998 B & H Publishing Group; Nashville,TN; pg 310-11
8. Community Bible Study Revelation Commentary by Timothy Crater, 1997-2004, Lesson 21, pg 5-6

CHAPTER 18

Chapter 18 opens with an angel's mighty voice proclaiming in verse 2, *"Fallen. Fallen is Babylon the Great."* From the excessive luxuries she gave herself, to the adulteries she committed and shared with others, we know that Babylon is a narcissistic, self-centered, self-indulgent place.

This reminds me of a story of a man who was driving his sports car along a winding road that had a steep embankment on one side. As he veered around a curve, he lost control and went over the cliff. The car came to a stop as it crashed against a boulder, throwing the man out. A motorist came along and found the man, dazed and bleeding profusely. He had lost his left arm in the crash. The helpful traveler was surprised to hear the man crying, "My car. My new car." The helper said, "Man, you have bigger problems. We've got to find your arm and get you to a hospital quickly." The man looked down, surprised, realized his arm was missing, and cried out, "My Rolex watch. My new Rolex watch." His priorities were all wrong.[1]

Babylon The Great

Babylon the Great will be a world trade center, a financial dream come true. The pursuit of riches will be the driving force of the city and its people. Trading, buying and selling will be valued even above human life. *slavery*

As the passage of scripture unfolds, there is an angel with great authority that comes down from heaven and announces that Babylon has fallen. The name 'Babylon' had come to epitomize the pagan, degenerate world in its political power, its moral decadence and its hostility to God and His people. In 18:5 it mentions that *"her sins are piled up to heaven, and God has remembered her crimes."* Contrast that with the way God sees us:

> *"For we are to God the pleasing aroma of Christ among those who are being saved and those who are perishing."*
>
> 2 Corinthians 2:15

If Babylon's sins are *"piled to heaven,"* and we who are with Christ are a *"pleasing aroma,"* can you just imagine the stench coming into heaven from Babylon? One commentator said this way:

> *"She [Babylon] is the hometown of earth's moral degradation and the prostitute of political power, the Madame of material excess and opulence."*[2]

All her relationships are evil and corrupt. According to scripture (18:2), she was *"a home for demons and a haunt for every evil spirit, a haunt for every unclean and detestable bird."* The very worst of demonic influences had settled there and had expressed themselves through the corrupt human behavior of the people who lived there. I'm sure this was a stench to God's nostrils!

Our daily choices determine whether we are growing spiritually or are piling up sins to the sky. We choose whether or not to covet. We choose whether or not to cheat or lie or steal. God pleads with us to run away from such corruption, just like He pleaded with His people in 18:4:

> *"Come out of her, my people, so that you will not share in her sins, so that you will not receive any of her plagues."*

Out of love for His own, God summons His people to leave the city for two important reasons:

1. To avoid its sins.
2. To avoid its destruction.

There is a Godly separation that has to happen if we are to not be harmed or defiled. Sometimes His protection comes from a sealing, but other times it comes from a complete removal. Remember Noah and the ark, or Lot and Sodom, or the tribulation saints? These are examples of His divine judgments. God has had enough of Babylon and He will now fill her cup generously with the wine of His wrath as mentioned in 16:17-20, and she will drink it *all.* Moreover, the measure of her "torture and grief" from God will be the same measure she used in lavishing herself with "glory and luxury," as He says in 18:7.

How this will happen is not said, but in today's world, we have the technology to destroy a city in one day with the use of nuclear weapons. Maybe Babylon the Great, will be nuked. Only God knows.

With the destruction of Babylon in one hour, I am reminded of the ancient city Pompeii in Southern Italy. It was built at the foot of Mt. Vesuvius and was totally destroyed when the mountain erupted in 79 A.D. In an instant it was covered by boiling lava and ash. Archaeologists recovered human bodies lying in beds or sitting at tables, with no warning at all. Through the sifting and digging, scientists have been able to recreate what life was like in that tragic city.

Just like the scientists of Pompeii - with the help of scripture and the Holy Spirit – we have been able to recreate what life will be like in the city of Babylon in the last days. Although Babylon will be a city of world power run by evil, it is already as dead as Pompeii.

God's prophesy always becomes man's history.

If the Lord were to start an excavation in your life, would you be happy with the picture that would be revealed in the layers? Would He find a house built on the foundation of Jesus, or would He find us camped out on the edge of Babylon?[4]

When I began chapter 17, I opened with a quote from St.Augustine, written over a thousand years ago:

> *"This city [of mankind] is earthly both in its beginning and in its end - a city in which nothing more is hoped for than can be seen in this world."*

> St. Augustine of Hippo
> "The City of God"

His book interpreted history as the story of two cities - the struggle between those who depend on God and those who rely on themselves. We know that the attitude from which the tower of Babel was built, was built on a dependence of oneself rather than a dependence on God. Remember the builders reasoned:[5]

> *"Let us build ourselves a city, with a tower that reaches to the heavens, so that we may make a name for ourselves."*

> Genesis 11:14

Dubai

The king of Dubai, Sheikh Mohammaed bin Rashid Al Maktoum, has referred to his city in a similar way. He began his reign as king in 2006 after the death of his brother. He is a billionaire many times over. Interestingly enough, Dubai is only about 30 years old as a city. Here's what is said about Dubai:

> "Dubai is a city in the United Arab Emirates known for luxury shopping, ultramodern architecture and a lively nightlife scene. Burj Khalifa, an 830m-tall tower, dominates the skyscraper-filled skyline. At its foot lies Dubai Fountain, with jets and lights choreographed to music. On man-made islands just offshore is Atlantis, the Palm, a resort with water and marine-animal parks."[6]

The Burj Khalifa is the tallest man-made building in the world today. Some say the architecture of the Burj Khalifa building is designed like the tower of Babel with its winding lines that go upward. I have found no article that states this as fact, just the speculation of others. But here's the reason I'm sharing this with you: I want to expand your minds for a moment and show you just how enticing a city can be, just how enticing Babylon the Great will be. Dubai is my closest example. I am not saying Dubai is Babylon, but I do want to point out how enticing this city can be. I want to encourage you to go to your computer and look up a promotional video on the city of Dubai. I know you'll be impressed, because it's an impressive city that can be mesmerizing and intoxicating.

While I don't believe Dubai to be "Babylon the Great," there are some similarities between it and the great city of Babylon. There is a dark side to this city. A few years back, the ABC news show, "20/20," did a story on Dubai and the slave industry. Here are a few tidbits from that episode:

- All those buildings were built by men in debtor's prison. They earned less than a dollar a day, so they'll never get out of debt. This then, is forced labor. They live in ghetto-type housing, all crammed in little rooms on the outskirts of the city. They cannot leave to go back home to their families because they are in debt, so they are forced to work.
- Sex trafficking is a huge business there. People are just commodities, not humans with souls.

- Man-made islands that look like palm trees from the air.
- Ousted leaders can hide there through their laws and still be able to live in opulence.
- Some hotel prices can range from $7,000 up to $11,000 a night for a suite.[7]

I'm not picking on Dubai. Most cities of this nature have a dark side. But with the opulence of this city and the enticing seductive flair of it, I wanted us to see that a Babylon *could* exist in our world today, in our lifetime.

What if this is a forerunner for Babylon? It is known for its drug trafficking and slave trading, a city rich in building and in prostitution. It is a rich city that the rich adore, and that world leaders love.

Babylon the Great may corrupt people in many different ways, from living a luxurious lifestyle at the expense of human misery to indulging in power for power's sake.

Studying this chapter should alert us to areas in our own lifestyle that may reflect a compromise with the world. Ask the Holy Spirit to show you if you have compromised yourself. Can the world tell the difference in the way you live and talk? Only you know the answer.

> *"Indeed the safest road to Hell is the gradual one--the gentle slope, soft underfoot, without sudden turnings, without milestones, without signposts,*
>
> *Your affectionate uncle, Screwtape."*
>
> C.S. Lewis
> The Screwtape Letters

Endnotes:

1. Community Bible Study TD Helps; 2009; Lesson 22; pg 59
2. Community Bible Study Revelation Commentary by Timothy Crater 1997-2004, Lesson 22, pg 3
3. Ibid., pg 3
4. Community Bible Study TD Helps; 2009; Lesson 22; pg 60
5. Kendall Easely, Revelation- Holman New Testament Commentary 1998 B & H Publishing Group; Nashville,TN; pg 303
6. https://www.google.com/search?q=Dubao&ie=utf-8&oe=utf-8
7. http://www.pbs.org/frontlineworld/rough/2007/09/dubai_sex_for_slinks.html

CHAPTER 19

C hapter 19 is about celebrations, invitations and feasts. There is a great shout of celebration which follows with a great feast. Hallelujah! The Great Tribulation has ended and Babylon has fallen. Babylon the Great, the harlot city, has been finally and *fully* judged.

John heard in verse 1 what sounded like the roar of a great multitude in heaven shouting. There was reason for this shouting. In verse 2 we find the answer:

1. *"He has condemned the great prostitute who corrupted the earth by her adulteries."*
2. *"He has avenged on her the blood of His servants."*

The shouts are for the permanent destruction of Babylon. Verse 3 offers proof of that permanence:

> *"The smoke from her goes up forever and ever."*

God has said before that vengeance is His to repay, not ours (Romans 12:19). It is only when God judges that the outcome is holy and true. He is avenging the saints and He is keeping His promise to them and to us. Evil is punished and righteousness triumphs. His Word is clear; we are not to attempt to take revenge against those who have wronged us. God will choose in His time to take that on, but we must trust in His timing and not ours, otherwise we make a mess of things for ourselves.

The first word John hears is, 'Hallelujah.' Hallelujah is defined as an exclamation of worship or a call to praise, translated from two Hebrew words meaning "Praise ye the Lord." Some Bible versions use the phrase *"Praise the Lord."* Hallelujah - *Praise You* ("Hallelu") - *Yahweh* ("jah").

Hallelujah in the Old Testament

Hallelujah is found 24 times in the Old Testament, but only in the book of Psalms. It appears in 15 different Psalms, between 104-150, and in almost every case at the opening and/or closing of the Psalm. These passages are called the *Hallelujah Psalms*. In Judaism, Psalms 113–118 are known as the *Hallel*, or *Hymn of Praise*. These verses are traditionally sung during Passover, the Feast of Pentecost, the Feast of Tabernacles and the Feast of Dedication.

Hallelujah in the New Testament

In the New Testament the term appears exclusively in Revelation 19:1-6. This is the only place it is used in the New Testament. The famous Handel's Messiah was written for this passage. Commentator Ken Easely had some good information about Handel and his *Messiah*, and I want to share his thoughts with you as it pertains to this chapter:

> *"Handel began to work on Messiah in 1741, using words from Scripture compiled by his friend Charles Jennens. He composed the music for all fifty-three numbers in an unbelievable twenty-four days. While audiences in the United States associate it with Christmas, in Handel's day Messiah was an Easter presentation, for the "Hallelujah." The chorus is not about Christmas, but about Christ's final victory. Jennens' words were taken from the only chapter that uses the word hallelujah, which is Revelation 19. "For the Lord God omnipotent reigneth" will come true in its fullest and most complete sense only at the mighty return of Jesus Christ in triumph."*[1]

In verse 4 we see the beautiful picture of the 24 Elders and the four living creatures who fall down and worship God, who was seated on the throne. Now comes the wedding feast.

Isaiah prophesied of a "great feast," a "banquet" following a great victory that the Lord had brought forth 700 years before Christ came.

> *On this mountain the Lord Almighty will prepare*
> *a feast of rich food for all peoples,*
> *a banquet of aged wine—*
> *the best of meats and the finest of wines. On this mountain he will*
> *destroy the shroud that enfolds all peoples,*
> *the sheet that covers all nations;*

He will swallow up death forever.
The Sovereign Lord will wipe away the tears from all faces;
He will remove his people's disgrace from all the earth.
The Lord has spoken.

Isaiah 25:6-8

In 19:4 the *"twenty-four elders and the four living creatures fell down and worshiped God."* As the great multitudes add their voices of praise and worship in the triumph, John describes the sound as being like the roar of rushing waters and loud peals of thunder. (19:6)

Another powerful Hallelujah rings out in heaven:

> *"The Lord God Almighty reigns, let us rejoice and be glad and give Him glory. For the wedding of the Lamb has come, and His bride has made herself ready."*

Revelation 19:7

I would like to quote Phyllis Cooper'sr commentary on this scripture:

> *"Just think about the mighty choir of all the saints of all times joined together in a shout of Hallelujah. With this wonderful word that crosses all language barriers, the church around the world sings praise to the Lord God Almighty. Hearing it sung at a church in a foreign land - or spoken by a believer from a different culture - draws us together in a Christian kinship with those whose language we do not understand. Someday we all will be together as part of that great choir; denominations will not matter, the color of our skin will be irrelevant, and cultural customs will be a thing of the past. All that will matter then is all that should matter now: God is triumphant. Jesus Christ reigns. The true church is one in Him. Hallelujah!"[2]*

The Lamb is Jesus. His bride is the church, who is prepared and clothed with the righteousness of Christ, put on by faith. She is further adorned with rewards given to her for righteous acts done in response to the salvation that was freely given to her by Jesus. Jesus and His church, His bride, will finally be united forever.

In Jewish weddings there were three phases to go through before the marriage was final:

1. Contract period: Payments of dowry; (they are legally married, but live apart).

2. Formal occasion: Groom takes the bride to his home.
3. Marriage supper: Groom comes to bride's home to feast.

This is what those three phases look like when the church is presented to Jesus:

1. Contract period: salvation. (The dowry has been paid.)
2. Formal occasion: rapture or death; (go home to be with the Lord).
3. Marriage supper: beginning event of the millennial reign of Jesus.[3]

Then the angel tells John:

> *"Blessed are those who are invited to the wedding supper of the Lamb."*

Revelation 19:9

From here on out, chapter 19 seems best divided into two feasts or suppers:

1. The Wedding Supper (The Feast of the Lamb)
2. The Great Supper of God

The Wedding Supper/The Feast of the Lamb

Those invited to the meal are truly privileged, for the Lamb wants them there, which means they share in His holiness and will therefore share in His kingdom.

Jesus told a parable in Matthew 22 of a king and his wedding feast:

> *Jesus spoke to them again in parables, saying: "The kingdom of heaven is like a king who prepared a wedding banquet for his son. He sent his servants to those who had been invited to the banquet to tell them to come, but they refused to come. Then he sent some more servants and said, 'Tell those who have been invited that I have prepared my dinner: My oxen and fattened cattle have been butchered, and everything is ready. Come to the wedding banquet.' But they paid no attention and went off - one to his field, another to his business. The rest seized his servants, mistreated them and killed them. The king was enraged. He sent his army and destroyed those murderers and burned their city. Then he said to his servants, 'The wedding banquet is ready, but those I invited did not deserve to come. So go to the street corners and invite to the banquet anyone*

you find.' So the servants went out into the streets and gathered all the people they could find, the bad as well as the good, and the wedding hall was filled with guests. But when the king came in to see the guests, he noticed a man there who was not wearing wedding clothes. He asked, 'How did you get in here without wedding clothes, friend?' The man was speechless. Then the king told the attendants, 'Tie him hand and foot, and throw him outside, into the darkness, where there will be weeping and gnashing of teeth.' For many are invited, but few are chosen."

Matthew 22:1-14

When the guests who were first invited refused, the king sent his servants to invite any others they could find. All are welcome, but there were two requirements:

1. Each had to accept the invitation.
2. Each had to wear wedding clothes.[4]

Anyone who sneaked in without proper attire was thrown out. It was customary for the king to provide the wedding garments. It makes sense, because:

"God made Him who had no sin to be sin for us, so that in Him we might become the righteousness of God."

2 Corinthians 5:21

We are clothed in the righteousness of Christ. This is our wedding garment. Christ our King has provided it for us. Not to be clothed in His righteousness would mean He died for nothing! This is a *gift*. Those who accept the Lamb's gracious invitation are transformed. We are a new creation.

"Therefore, if anyone is in Christ, the new creation has come: The old has gone, the new is here."

2 Corinthians 5:17

As the scene opens in 19:11, the doors to heaven stand open. There He is. He first came as an infant, meek and mild. This time He comes as King of kings and LORD of lords - faithful and true. His promises ring true as He appears in His return. He is powerful and just. He is the Word of God, coming to make war and to judge the unbelieving world with the sword of His mouth, the sword of God's Word. He is faithful. God's Word never comes back void...*ever*.

There, visibly written on His robe and on His thigh, is the title:

KING OF KINGS AND LORD OF LORDS

This is recalling Moses' declaration to the nation of Israel:

> *"For the Lord your God is God of gods and Lord of lords, the great God, mighty and awesome, who shows no partiality and accepts no bribes."*
>
> Deuteronomy 10:17

All such titles proclaim God's utter, universal sovereignty; absolutely none is higher. He has always possessed such authority, but now He is asserting it completely over the entire planet to establish God's kingdom on earth.[5]

As soldiers of the Lord, we live inside enemy territory. Our mission is to witness by word and by deed, and through that, we make disciples of Jesus.

This passage tells us that one day we will no longer be the aliens, because Jesus is coming again, and the kingdom of the Earth will become His Kingdom. The tables will be turned. We will be citizens living under Christ's reign. This hope should focus our lives and our witness.

Time is short and people need to hear the Good News of Jesus Christ. Let's invite all to come to the wedding feast and put on the wedding garments provided for us. Accept His invitation.

The Great Supper of God

In 19:17 an angel stands in the sun, and cries in a loud voice to the birds flying in midair. This is for all the birds to hear and to respond. They are invited to *"the great supper of God"* (19:17).

Earlier in John's vision, Jesus is given the scroll, and it was to be opened for Him to ultimately judge the earth. Judgment has come. Some Old Testament passages foresee a great time of slaughter of God's enemies. In Isaiah 34, God speaks to His people about His anger against the nations that will come.

> *"The sword of the Lord is bathed in blood,*
> *it is covered with fat - the blood of lambs and goats,*
> *fat from the kidneys of rams. For the Lord has a sacrifice in Bozrah and a great slaughter in the land of Edom."*
>
> Isaiah 34:6

In Revelation 19:18, nowhere else is there such a gory picture as the birds devouring:

> *"...the flesh of kings, generals, mighty men, horses and their riders, and the flesh of all people, free and slave, small and great."*

This is a stark contrast of what we just read about the wonderful and joyful wedding feast. Who are these people? Where did they come from?

Revelation 6:15 tells us:

> *"Then the kings of the earth, the princes, the generals, the rich, the mighty, and every slave and every free man hid in caves and among the rocks of the mountains."*

These are the people of hardened hearts, who cursed God in every way. Here is the winepress of God's wrath. This becomes a worldwide catastrophe with a huge river of blood. This could be the fulfillment of what was spoken in chapter 14.

> *"The angel swung his sickle on the earth, gathered its grapes and threw them into the great winepress of God's wrath. They were trampled in the winepress outside the city, and blood flowed out of the press, rising as high as the horses' bridles for a distance of 1,600 stadia"* (180 miles long).

Revelation 14:19-20

Remember, what we learned earlier:

1. One-third of the human race suffered death by plague.
2. Millions more had perished with the outpouring of the first four bowls.
3. But now we have the surviving two-thirds that have a date with death because they thought they could defeat God Almighty.

It's incredible that people still choose to wage war against Almighty God. When we decide in any way, shape or form that we are in control, we are waging war against God.[6] I like the Contemporary English Version translation of Job 11:13-15:

> *"Surrender your heart to God, turn to Him in prayer, and give up your sins, even those you do in secret. Then you won't be ashamed; you will be confident and fearless."*

Be in a state of surrender to Him. Keep your heart in check and don't wage war against God.

When the fall of Babylon and the end times' signs begin, it is possible it will not be a supernatural event. I'm not saying it won't, I'm just saying it's quite possible the unbelieving world will explain it away somehow with logic or science.

For example:

- A meteorite hitting the earth could be one of the judgments.
- Dubai could be just the beginning of these types of cities (the spirit of Babylon is already here).
- The increase in beheadings may not just be because of militant groups like ISIS, or other terrorist organizations.
- Sex trafficking and slave trading is already here and on the rise.

The political climate is changing, but we as Christians, need to know and understand our scripture. We need to be familiar with what the Word of God says, the prophecies foretold, and focus on the One who deserves all praise and worship. We need to trust *Who* is in control and what this all means. Otherwise, we could cave in to fear of what our eyes see and take matters into our own hands and end up in a position of worshipping the antichrist and receive the mark of the beast!

More importantly, we will miss chances to help others come to understand just *who* Jesus Christ really *is* and to enter eternity with Him. Do we really want to enter these times *without* an understanding of what God has revealed to us through scripture?

Pastor Don Finto is a beloved pastor all around the world. His book, "PREPARE. For The End Time Harvest" is an informative book that cites current events happening from across the nations. He cross references scripture upon scripture regarding Jesus' teaching of the parable of the wheat and the weeds growing together. He gives much insight to the prophecies about Israel and their fulfillment. Many have already been fulfilled. God is speaking to us, we just have to see and hear, and listen to what the Holy Spirit is revealing. We are not to be blind to this, but to be prepared.[7]

Some of this is happening slowly; so slow we may not recognize it. We may make things too logical in our minds because our hearts have become jaded and hardened. We have become too busy with our lives and livelihoods to recognized God speaking to us daily through His Word.

This is a graphic example, but the best one I know:

- If we know that there are saints that will be beheaded for not giving in or renouncing our faith, then ask yourself, would you be able to go through that? It's happening now, and Jesus hasn't even returned yet.
- Would you choose to not feed your family because it meant taking the mark of the beast to get money to do so? Your heart will be tested. God's Word is very clear here.
- Do you trust in your 401(k) or your possessions more than you trust in God? That doesn't protect you. You have to be alert and wise to the Word and follow what it says to do.

This time period will be harder than we think. If we don't know and understand what scripture says and what it means when we look all around us, we will be tempted to fall because satan is the great deceiver. Some of you feel you will be taken to heaven and not have to deal with any of this during the tribulation. That may be true, but scripture is not 100% clear on this. No one knows for sure. I encourage us all to keep in check our heart's priorities and keep our eyes on Jesus, who will lead us because He loves us.

I'm not trying to scare you. That type of fear does not come from the Lord above. But I am trying to wake you up to see the importance of getting involved with the Word more. In this ever changing world that we live in today, we need to know how to live and how not to be deceived. That is why I keep reminding you of Who is in control. We can't look at life through just our earthly eyes. Life needs to be viewed through spiritual eyes as well, which brings peace, *a peace that surpasses all understanding.* (Philippians 4:7)

Now, back to chapter 19.

We come to the great battle scene: the beast and the kings of the earth and their armies gather together to make war against the rider on the horse and his army. We are poised for The Battle of Armageddon. While this epic battle has been mythologized in films and by popular fiction, the reality as described by John as more of an anti-climax than a climax.

Poof!

The battle is over before the battle even begins.

The war at the end of the world never really materializes. John puts it simply in 19:20:

"*The beast was captured, and with him the false prophet.*"

This is the end of their story. The beast and the false prophet are thrown alive into the fiery lake of burning sulfur. There is no judgment for them, just a sentence. And that sentence is hell itself - *forever*.

John's description of the false prophet reminds us how vile this monster really is:

> *"But the beast was captured, and with it the false prophet who had performed the signs on its behalf. With these signs he had deluded those who had received the mark of the beast and worshiped its image. The two of them were thrown alive into the fiery lake of burning sulfur."*

> Revelation 19:20

There is no battle. They are just tossed away, no longer to deceive anyone ever again. With the ring-leader and his mouthpiece gone, the enemy armies are all that's left on the battlefield.

The casualties of war are those who are deceived. Those who lead others into sin are subject to a more severe punishment. In Mark 9:42-43 Jesus warns:

> *"If anyone causes one of these little ones - those who believe in Me - to stumble, it would be better for them if a large millstone were hung around their neck and they were thrown into the sea."*

We know that the beast, dragon and the false prophet have such power in their deception that even kings and armies will follow them. In Daniel 11, Daniel has a vision that predicts that kings and their armies will be fighting each other and then turn to fight against God and His people. (Daniel 11:36-45)

One way to avoid being a casualty of the deceiver is to stay in the truth. Draw near to the Word, the Word that was made flesh, who is our Lord and Savior, Jesus Christ. He is faithful and true. Seek Him so you won't be a casualty of war.

This is the first time in Scripture that the final place of punishment for the wicked is described as *"the fiery lake of burning sulfur."*

Mark must have known something about hell being a fiery place because the rest of the scripture warning says this:

> *"If your hand causes you to stumble, cut it off. It is better for you to enter life maimed than with two hands to go into hell, where the fire never goes out."*

> Mark 9:42-43

There are people who believe that hell is not a real place, that it is just something religious authority figures use to scare people into 'being good or submissive.' Do not be deceived. According to this scripture, hell is a very real place of torment for the wicked.

The kings and the rest of the armies are killed with the sword that comes out of the Jesus' mouth. Jesus is true power. He spoke the world into existence and He can speak to destroy the wicked too. The last sentence of this chapter completes their end.

> *"The birds gorged themselves on their flesh."*
>
> Revelation 19:21

In the book of Daniel, which was written nearly 2,500 years ago, an exiled prophet stood before a king who had a troubling dream. King Nebuchadnezzar of Babylon dreamed of a great statue made of various metals which was destroyed by a mighty rock. Daniel, interpreting its meaning, described the metals as the kingdoms to follow Babylon. He finishes his interpretation:

> *"The God of heaven will set up a kingdom that will never be destroyed, nor will it be left to another people. It will crush all those kingdoms and bring them to an end, but it will itself endure forever. This is the meaning of the vision of the rock cut out of a mountain, but not by human hands—a rock that broke the iron, the bronze, the clay, the silver and the gold to pieces" The kings response: "Surely your God is the God of gods and the Lord of kings and a revealer of mysteries, for you were able to reveal this mystery."* [8]
>
> Daniel 2:46-47

May we acknowledge Jesus Christ as the God of gods and the Lord of kings for ourselves.

He deserves our worship and our praise. He is worthy of it all!

Endnotes:

1. Kendall Easely, Revelation- Holman New Testament Commentary 1998 B & H Publishing Group; Nashville,TN; pg 345
2. Community Bible Study Revelation commentary by Phyllis Coope,r 1997-2004, Lesson 23, pg 4
3. Community Bible Study TD Helps; 2009; Lesson 22; pg 62-63
4. Community Bible Study Revelation commentary by Timothy Crater, 1997-2004, Lesson 23, pg 6
5. Ibid., Lesson 24 pg 4
6. Kendall Easely, Revelation- Holman New Testament Commentary 1998 B & H Publishing Group; Nashville,TN; pg 356
7. PREPARE. For The End-Time Harvest, copyright 2015 by Don Finto, Published by Caleb Publications
8. Community Bible Study Revelation commentary by Phyllis Coope,r 1997-2004, Lesson 23, pg 8

Chapter 20

Now John witnesses satan, who is both the devil and the accuser of the brethren, being jailed in the Abyss. The word comes from the Greek root word "bythos" for bottom. The word "alpha" is for "the," so it should read "the bottom." But it doesn't. It just says Abyss, explaining that this is a "bottomless" place.[1] Now he is shackled and locked away in there.

John calls him by four names here:

1. The dragon; a reference to his description in chapter 12 as *"an enormous red dragon"* who made war against the saints.
2. That ancient serpent; a reference to his serpentine seduction of Adam and Eve in the Garden of Eden, where the destruction and grief he caused among men began.
3. The devil; means slanderer or accuser, and is especially descriptive of his accusations against the saints.
4. The adversary, satan, opposer of God, His people and His works.[2]

Yes, he has other names too, but these four names give the essence of his wretched work on earth, and he is now bound for 1,000 years in the bottomless pit.

The Thousand Years

There are differing views that Christians have about the 1,000 year period. The most basic question is whether this is a literal and earthly period of a 1,000 years or a spiritual symbol of the triumph of God over evil in eternity. Those who trust in Christ for eternal life, hold several views on the kingdom and on the specific teachings about it in this chapter. Since these differences do not affect the good news of the gospel (salvation by grace through faith), sincere believers have agreed to disagree on this question.

Here are three schools of thought (simply put) on the earthly reign of Christ:

1. Amillennial - No literal reign on earth; Christ's reign is in the hearts of believers.
2. Postmillennial - Jesus comes after the triumph of the Gospel. Things just get better and better then heaven on earth prompts Jesus to return.
3. Premillennial - Jesus returns, and then there is a 1,000 year reign on earth. Revelation 20:1-6 is about Jesus' reign on Earth. He will reign there for 1,000 years and His saints will rule with Him.[3]

Every position that Christians hold on prophecy has its weak points and strong points. No one view has all the right answers. As believers, each of us is responsible for studying God's Word, praying for the Holy Spirit's wisdom, and then finding your view that is best supported by scripture.

I am here to share information - not to tell you what to believe. If there is question that won't leave you alone about this, ask your Pastor for some guidance and help, but more importantly, seek the scriptures for yourself and ask the Holy Spirit to teach you.

I share the Premillennial view point, and teach from that perspective.

According to John, during Christ's thousand year reign on earth, satan will not be able to deceive the nations (he is bound in the Abyss, remember?).

Perhaps you might be asking yourself, as I did when I first read this passage; 'why doesn't God simply destroy satan and be done with it!?' Well… we are not told why. But God has His purposes and He is not obligated to reveal them to us. Psalm 115:3 (NASB) explains it this way:

> *"But our God is in the heavens; He does whatever He pleases."*

John sees another image after satan is bound and imprisoned.

> *"I saw thrones on which were seated those who had been given authority to judge. And I saw the souls of those who had been beheaded because of their testimony about Jesus and because of the word of God. They had not worshiped the beast or its image and*

had not received its mark on their foreheads or their hands. They came to life and reigned with Christ a thousand years."

Revelation 20:4

The thrones are for all the saints that are given authority to judge. Who are they? No one knows for sure, but most agree it is probably the 12 apostles and the 24 elders, the armies of Christ, and John's special focus, the Tribulation martyrs:

"The armies of heaven were following Him, riding on white horses and dressed in fine linen, white and clean."

Revelation19:14

They are also the souls of tribulation saints, the witnesses for Christ and the Word of God:

"...of those who had been beheaded because of their testimony for Jesus and because of the Word of God."

Revelation 20:4

They overcame and there is a special reward for them befitting their sacrifice. These are the souls that were under the altar in Revelation 6:9, slain for *"the word of God and the testimony they had maintained,"* being raised, vindicated and exalted. They kept their faith and testimony in the face of suffering and death. Now they will reign with Christ during this 1,000 year period.

God has made promises to believers who overcome. This should inspire us to keep our faith in Christ regardless of what may happen to us.

"Or do you not know that the Lord's people will judge the world?

1 Corinthians 6:2

"If we suffer, we shall also reign with Him."

2 Timothy 2:12

"To him who overcomes and does My will to the end, I will give authority over the nations."

Revelation 2:26

"To the one who is victorious, I will give the right to sit with me on my throne, just as I was victorious and sat down with my Father on his throne."

Revelation 3:21

And in Daniel, he was told this in his vision:

"And the kingdom and dominion, and the greatness of the kingdom under the whole heaven, shall be given to the people of the saints of the most High"

Daniel 7:27

He see's these souls come to life and reign (20:4b), meaning their spirits/souls, which were in heaven, were joined to their re-created and resurrected bodies at Christ's coming so they could live and reign on earth with Him.[4] When all of this takes place is a matter of interpretation and much conjecture. But this marks the time of the millennial kingdom, and this is considered the first resurrection, as stated in 20:5.

Then John adds that, *"the rest of the dead did not come to life until the thousand years were ended."* Now, verse five of this chapter is one of the hardest verses to decipher.

John's statement that *"...the rest of the dead did not come to life until the thousand years were ended"* is best treated as something written in parentheses. The word translated as "come to life" is the Greek word "ezesan," which is also used of the resurrection of the martyrs in the verse before (20:4).

Jesus Himself taught that both the just and unjust must rise to meet their fates. The unjust have to wait until after the thousand years have past.[6]

"Do not be amazed at this, for a time is coming when all who are in their graves will hear his voice and come out - those who have done what is good will rise to live, and those who have done what is evil will rise to be condemned."

John 5:28-29

Those in the first resurrection will enjoy the kingdom of God; *"over such the second death has no power over them"* (20:6). The second death refers to the lake of fire where the wicked are sent after the final judgment (20:14). This is a place of complete separation from God and a permanent existence under His wrath.

Let's be clear here and let no fear in and have no doubt where you are going. For if you are scared because you are not sure, then listen to Timothy Crater's words. He explains this well:

"No believer in Christ will ever stand at the Great White Throne Judgment (20:11-15), and thus will never be in danger of the lake of fire, the second death. All true believers will be raised at the

beginning of the kingdom. We will never see the lake of fire; it has no power over us (20:6). Far from suffering the second death in the lake of fire, believers raised at the Second Coming will be priests of God and of Christ, occupying honored, privileged positions before the Godhead with access to the divine presence. More than that, we will "reign with Him for a thousand years" (20:6). We will be priests and we will be kings, as promised in Revelation 1:6 and 5:10."

"...and has made us to be a kingdom and priests to serve his God and Father - to him be glory and power forever and ever. Amen."

Revelation 1:6

"You have made them to be a kingdom and priests to serve our God, and they will reign on the earth."

Revelation 5:10

"We will function both as holy, sanctified servants before God and as governmental officials exercising rule over men on God's behalf."

To summarize:

- 1,000 years marks the length of time that satan is bound.
- Nations are free from his deception.
- Saints will reign with Christ.
- The wicked must wait to come to judgment. That is called the second death and it is for them.[7]

It is during this time that all the great Old Testament prophecies about a glorious messianic rule will be fulfilled.

"He will judge between the nations and will settle disputes for many peoples. They will beat their swords into plowshares and their spears into pruning hooks. Nation will not take up sword against nation, nor will they train for war anymore."

Isaiah 2:4

"The wolf will live with the lamb, the leopard will lie down with the goat, the calf and the lion and the yearling together; and a little child will lead them.
The cow will feed with the bear, their young will lie down together, and the lion will eat straw like the ox. The infant will play near the cobra's den, and the young child will put its hand into the viper's nest. They will neither harm nor destroy on all my holy

mountain, for the earth will be filled with the knowledge of the Lord as the waters cover the sea."

Isaiah 11: 6-9

Isaiah describes God's kingdom of righteousness here (I just love this).

"The fruit of that righteousness will be peace; its effect will be quietness and confidence forever. My people will live in peaceful dwelling places, in secure home in undisturbed places of rest."

Isaiah 32:17-18

It sounds so lovely compared to what we live with today. I anticipate this with much joy. In my opinion, these Old Testament attributes of Christ and His reign mentioned in Isaiah 32 are similar to the New Testament fruits of the Spirit of *"love, joy, peace, patience, kindness, goodness, faithfulness, gentleness and self-control."*

Even though we are not in heaven yet with Christ, we need to remember, this is not our home. But this can be a happy place for us to live if we use these attributes of the Spirit for living in the kingdom now, today. As we age, and our earthly bodies begin to fail us, we can thank God that such glory lies ahead.

The Final Rebellion

The book of Revelation gives us specific details not only about the kingdom of God, but also about the end of satan. At Christ's return and His establishment of His kingdom, God does not get rid of all evil yet or the evil doers.

His plan seems to be done in phases. Between the two phases of God's kingdom comes the last phase of evil - an inspired rebellion, motivated by satan.

He [satan], is released after the thousand years are over and he does what he does best, deceive. He gathers those who have acted like they believe in Christ, but aren't true believers.

The assumption from this and other scripture is that the millennial kingdom will consist both of the resurrected saints in immortal resurrected bodies, and people living in mortal bodies on the earth from which the curse has been lifted. Under Christ's rule, people will still have sin natures, but will be spared satan's temptations and seductions for a time.

Daniel 7:11-12 offers an explanation:

> *"Then I continued to watch because of the boastful words the horn was speaking. I kept looking until the beast was slain and its body destroyed and thrown into the blazing fire. (The other beasts had been stripped of their authority, but were allowed to live for a period of time.)"*

The other beasts signifies other kingdoms according to Daniel's vision. They will be allowed to enter Christ's kingdom, but they will forfeit their ruling positions to the saints.

Daniel 7:27 goes on to say:

> *"Then the sovereignty, power and greatness of all the Kingdoms under heaven will be handed over to the holy people of the Most High. His kingdom will be an everlasting kingdom, and all rulers will worship and obey him."*[8]

The tragedy of the final rebellion by the deceived ones is that during the Millennium, they lived in a perfect environment. They appeared to be obedient and submissive to God, but just as Jeremiah 17:9 says:

> *"The heart is deceitful above all things and beyond cure. Who can understand it?"*

A perfect environment cannot produce a perfect heart. These people are not real believers, but posers, people who pretend what they are not. And these posers rebel and make themselves into a formidable force, which surrounds the city of God, the camp of God's people, which is Jerusalem.[9]

Gog and Magog are first mentioned in Ezekiel chapters 38-39. Ezekiel is given a prophecy about Jerusalem and an impending war against them. Gog is an evil prince, and Magog is his distant land or territory, or his people of the land ("Ma" means "land").

> *"Son of man, set your face against Gog, of the land of Magog, the chief prince of Meshek and Tubal; prophesy against him."*
>
> Ezekiel 38:2

Some of you may know that the names Magog, Meshek and Tubal were the names of Japheth's son's and Japheth was one of the sons of Noah. The names became tribes that settled in various lands. Commentaries are all over the place about finding significance with all of this, but none are clear. I feel we can get off of the point of what this chapter's message is, if we try to untangle all of this with these names and why God chose those names. Nothing is clear. Except that these names symbolize the nations of the world as they band together for the final assault on God.

The prophecy in Ezekiel 38 speaks of an invasion against Israel as she dwells in peace.

> *"Therefore, son of man, prophesy and say to Gog: This is what the Sovereign Lord says: 'In that day, when my people Israel are living in safety, will you not take notice of it? You will come from your place in the far north, you and many nations with you, all of them riding on horses, a great horde, a mighty army. You will advance against my people Israel like a cloud that covers the land. In days to come, Gog, I will bring you against my land, so that the nations may know me when I am proved holy through you before their eyes.'"*

Ezekiel 38:14-16

And God will send fire on Magog. Ezekiel 39:6 says:

> *"I will send fire on Magog and on those who live in safety in the coastlands, and they will know that I am the Lord."*

John's brief description in Revelation parallels that of Ezekiel's prophecy and portrayal of the millennium. This is not a minor rebellion. In 20:8 it says their numbers are like *"sand on the seashore."* This will be hordes and hordes of rebellion against God.[10]

It's so sad to think that even in a perfect environment, ruled by a perfect King who is Christ Himself, people will choose to go their own destructive way and satan will succeed all the way to his end, deceiving people who know who God is.

This rebellion is like an intoxication toward their leader, satan, and they have grandiose delusions of victory. They have come from afar and have surrounded Jerusalem, *"the city He [God] loves."* (20:9)

God has had enough of the rebellion now. These rebels have seen Christ, and have lived under His divine rule in His peaceable kingdom. He loves all His children, but they have made their choice; and now God must make His. He does not negotiate with them, speak to them, or even attack them in battle. He simply incinerates them, just like Ezekiel 39 prophesied.

> *"...fire came down from heaven and devoured them."*

Revelation 20:9

Those who die at this point will be the last mortals to die...*forever.* Human rebellion has ended.

As for satan's end, John states his eternal destiny in 20:10:

> *"The devil, who deceived them, was thrown into the lake of burning sulfur."*

In Matthew 25:41, Jesus speaks about this:

> *"Then He will say to those on His left, 'Depart from Me, you who are cursed, into the eternal fire prepared for the devil and his angels.'"*

There is no standing before God to await judgment. The adversary, satan, is thrown into the lake of fire, just like the antichrist and his false prophet were. We learn from 20:10 that they *"will be tormented day and night forever and ever."*

Interesting point I'd like to make: They do not cease to exist; they go on existing in pain and torment. Their annihilation would actually be an act of mercy, but they had shown none to others, and will therefore receive none themselves. The enemy's part in their fate is one reason satan is due such a severe eternal punishment.[11]

Remember what God has said, in Deuteronomy 32:35 and Romans 12:19:

> *"It is Mine to avenge; I will repay..."*

His promises are *yes* and *amen.* God's judgment is just and righteous.

The Final Judgment

This chapter reminds me of what happens when a case goes all the way to the Supreme Court to be heard. The court has the right to announce a refusal to even hear it. In fact, on October 3, 1994, when the U.S. Supreme Court began its 1994-95 term, according to the New York Times, they refused to hear more than 1,600 cases. This was the final word. There were no arguments. Just, *No.* The books are sealed on the cases and doors shut. This was the final word.

John teaches that one day the Supreme Court of the universe, with Chief Justice Jesus at the throne, will sit in final judgment.[12]

During Jesus' earthly ministry He taught about His Second Coming. He connected kingship closely with judging.[13]

> *"When the Son of Man comes in His glory, and all the angels with Him, He will sit on His throne in heavenly glory. All the nations will be gathered before Him, He will separate the people one from another as a shepherd separates the sheep from the goats."*
>
> Matthew 25:31-32

The Great White Throne appears, but from this passage it is not clear who sits on the throne. We actually find this elsewhere in scripture and it is crystal clear it is Jesus Christ.

> *"Moreover, the Father judges no one, but has entrusted all judgment to the Son, that all may honor the Son just as they honor the Father. Whoever does not honor the Son does not honor the Father, who sent him."*
>
> John 5:22-23

Christ as judge is so unimaginably great, so awesome in power and might that the earth and sky flee from His presence (20:11). This marks the disappearing of an old universe to make way for a new heaven. But before the new heaven and earth can appear, the Great Judgment must occur.

The Great Judgment

After the old heaven and earth disappear, the dead are raised. They come to life at the end of the thousand year period. As we have learned, this is the second resurrection.

Let's review so we have some context here. The first resurrection is found in Revelation 20:4-5:

> *"I saw thrones on which were seated those who had been given authority to judge. And I saw the souls of those who had been beheaded because of their testimony about Jesus and because of the word of God. They had not worshiped the beast or its image and had not received its mark on their foreheads or their hands. They came to life and reigned with Christ a thousand years. (The rest of the dead did not come to life until the thousand years were ended.) This is the first resurrection."*

The contrast between the two resurrections is an overall negative tone. It seems to suggest that the Great White Throne Judgment is the judgment of the lost. These people were not blessed and holy.

It also seems there are two kinds of books from which God will judge from. There is a set of books (plural in 20:12) that likely hold the record of each human's thoughts, words and deeds throughout mortal life. These books will probably cover both sins that we fail to do, and the sins that we often do, and all the secret sins in between.

> *"If anyone, then, knows the good they ought to do and doesn't do it, it is sin for them."*
>
> James 4:17

> *"But I tell you that everyone will have to give account on the day of judgment for every empty word they have spoken."*
>
> Matthew 12: 36

> *"I the Lord search the heart and examine the mind, to reward each person according to their conduct, according to what their deeds deserve."*
>
> Jeremiah 17: 10

God has an absolute standard to judge with - His righteousness. He will not grade on a curve, nor will He give points for good behavior. He is not politically correct either. He is just and righteous and He will judge accordingly. Romans 3:10, 23 reminds us that:

> *"...there is no one righteous, not even one...for all have sinned and fall short of the glory of God."*

Then another book was opened, which was the book of life (verses 20:12b).

It is a singular book, possibly because it lists only names and not deeds. This is the Lamb's Book of Life which is referenced in Revelation chapter 21. The books are opened, and judgment is given. Now, here's the good news. If you come in faith, your books have been balanced; His account is credited to yours. The bad news is, if you have no faith, only works, you are judged only on your own merit. And the verdict will be guilty.[14]

We serve a just and merciful God. He demands righteousness and He provides it for all who by faith receive Jesus as Savior. When you receive Jesus, you receive His righteousness; your account is cleared, your debt is paid, reconciled.

Thank God for His Grace. Apart from this, judgment will be swift and it will be *final*.

Romans 6:23 says the wages of sin is death. Payday is here for those who refused to know and believe in Him. After the judgment of unbelievers is passed, the sentence is carried out. Death and Hades are destroyed. The convicted and the condemned are thrown into the lake of fire for eternity. They are eternally separated from God, eternally separated from the new life in the new heaven and earth. Verse 20:14 describes the second death, and it is brutal.

Remember though, it has no power over saints, over the tribulation martyrs, or over those who follow the Lamb. It is a final place the unbeliever will go - an infernal sea of torment more ghastly than anything any human could imagine.

Painful torment is what we are saved from and it explains the extreme measures God and Christ took to provide our salvation.

Remember, though God is love, He is also righteous, pure and holy. No sinful person will be able to live with Him in eternity. He is sinless, therefore He cannot co-exist with sin. Out of His love He has provided a way to deal with sin, so we can be united with Him through faith in Jesus Christ. Don't let doubt sink in and tell you there are other ways and other religions. All ways do not lead you to heaven. There is only one way and that is through believing in Jesus Christ as your Savior. Scripture is clear here; Jesus says:

> *"I am the way and the truth and the life. No one comes to the Father except through Me."*
>
> John 14:6

There is a hell. A lot of people think Christians have made this up to scare everyone and that there really isn't a hell. But scripture says it is a place, a real place - and sadly it will be filled with people who were deceived in this life. They will be judged and separated from God. Eternal torment is a frightening reality - separation from God and His goodness and hope… I keep thinking of the darkness in the Mammoth caves I experienced. It all makes me shutter.

The burning lake is an awful eternal reality that Christ died to *save* mankind *from experiencing.*

Won't you take a moment and except Jesus as your Savior if you haven't already? This is a serious book with a serious subject - eternal life or eternal damnation. Are you willing to gamble with your soul? Jesus is *real* and He is all powerful and mighty. Accept Him as your Savior now and begin to watch your life change for the better. He loves you so much!

Here's an illustration I found that fits the closing of this chapter;

> *"An article in the National Geographic Magazine told of a great fire in Yellowstone Park several years ago. After the fire, a park ranger walked through the park to assess the damage. At the base of a tree, he found a dead bird—literally petrified in ashes, like a statue on the ground. The ranger poked the bird with a stick, and three tiny chicks scurried from under their mother's wings—Alive. She could have flown away and lived, but her babies would have died. She gave up her life in the fire, so those under the cover of her wings could live."*[5]

Hear the cries of Jesus' heart as He said these words in Luke 13:34:

> *"Jerusalem, Jerusalem, you who kill the prophets and stone those sent to you, how often I have longed to gather your children together, as a hen gathers her chicks under her wings, and you were not willing."*

If you have received Jesus, then you are saved. If you've never received Jesus as your personal Savior, or if you're not sure, receive Him now. He has passed through the fire for you and He longs to gather you under His wings of His grace and mercy.

If you have read all of chapter 20 and come away from it unmoved, then you have misread it. We must take a moment and ponder that we too, all of us, will face an eternal Judge one day. Are we living a life with that in mind?[16]

Old Hymns have such power and meaning. This old hymn was written by Edward Mote in the 1800's and was called "My Hope Is Built On Nothing Less," then years later when William B. Bradbury added the music, it was called "Solid Rock." Read through these lyrics, especially the third stanza and remember this chapter. If you know the melody, I pray it brings you hope and helps you find your way through to Christ. Build your life on the Solid Rock of Jesus Christ.

"My Hope Is Built On Nothing Less" / "The Solid Rock"

> *My hope is built on nothing less*
> *Than Jesus' blood and righteousness;*
> *I dare not trust the sweetest frame,*
> *But wholly lean on Jesus' name.*
>
> *On Christ, the solid Rock, I stand;*

All other ground is sinking sand,
All other ground is sinking sand.

When darkness veils His lovely face,
I rest on His unchanging grace;
In every high and stormy gale,
My anchor holds within the veil.

His oath, His covenant, His blood
Support me in the whelming flood;
When all around my soul gives way,
He then is all my hope and stay.

When He shall come with trumpet sound,
Oh, may I then in Him be found;
Dressed in His righteousness alone,
Faultless to stand before the throne.

Endnotes:

1. Community Bible Study TD Helps; 2009; Lesson 25; pg 67
2. Ibid pg., 66
3. Ibid pg., 66
4. Community Bible Study Revelation, by Timothy Crater 1997-2004, Lesson 25 pg 5
5. Ibid. pg., 5
6. Ibid. pg., 6
7. Ibid. pg., 7
8. Ibid. Les. 26 pg 2
9. Community Bible Study TD Helps; 2009; Lesson 26; pg 68
10. Community Bible Study Revelation, by Timothy Crater 1997-2004, Lesson 26, pg 2
11. Community Bible Study TD Helps; 2009; Lesson 26; pg 68
12. Kendall Easely, Revelation- Holman New Testament Commentary 1998 B & H Publishing Group; Nashville,TN; pg 379
13. Community Bible Study Revelation, by Timothy Crater 1997-2004, Lesson 26, pg 4
14. Ibid. pg., 5-6
15. Community Bible Study TD Helps; 2009; Lesson 26; pg 69
16. Kendall Easely, Revelation- Holman New Testament Commentary 1998 B & H Publishing Group; Nashville,TN; pg 384
17. Edward Mote, "My Hope Is Built On Nothing Less" copyright 1834, William B. Bradbury, "Solid Rock" copyright 1863, Public Domain

CHAPTER 21

"Heaven is the perfectly ordered and harmonious enjoyment of God and of one another in God."

Augustine of Hippo

In about 950 B.C., the earthly city of Jerusalem reached its most magnificent expression. Solomon, the wisest king in the world, ruled as the son of David. The temple in all its glory stood as a testament to Israel's God. This was the golden age for Jerusalem. Dignitaries such as the Queen of Sheba came seeking Solomon's counsel and bringing him gifts of the greatest of treasures.

After Solomon's death, his kingdom was divided, split in two, each dead set against the other. Idol worship returned and the people fell away from God once again. The temple was torched by the Babylonians in 586 B.C., and the memory of this golden age burned fiercely in the hearts of the Jewish people.

Almost 3,000 years later, that same memory still lives. The blue Star of David is the central feature of the modern Israeli flag. Jerusalem is again the center of Israel's life.

John's vision of the New Jerusalem in chapter 21, surpasses the old Jerusalem of Solomon, just as a diamond surpasses a rhinestone.[1] John was given multiple visions concerning the very end of time. These are what he has seen in the last few chapters so far:

- The prostitute city's doom (Ch. 17-18).
- The Wedding was announced (Ch. 19-20).
- Judgment and a brief scene of the Holy bride city (Ch.20).

And now, John is ushered into the fourth and final vision of the bride city in detail, and the portrait of Jesus among His people throughout eternity.

It is a relief after the solemn judgment scene of the Great White Throne, the scene of the New Jerusalem. What he saw, however, transcends anything that could exist in the universe as we now understand it.

"And there was no longer the sea..."

Revelation 21:1

Commentators differ in their understanding of what the absence of the sea implies.

- The sea was a metaphor for the wicked. *"But the wicked are like the tossing sea, which cannot rest, whose waves cast up mire and mud."* Isaiah 57:20
- The first great monster came from there. *"The dragon stood on the shore of the sea. And I saw a beast coming out of the sea. It had ten horns and seven heads, with ten crowns on its horns, and on each head a blasphemous name."* Revelation 13:1
- It divides people. God will remove everything that separates His people from one another. Beyond that, the earth will no longer need the cleansing properties of salt water. Pollution and sin are a thing of the past. God's provision will be perfect.

The only water that will exist will be a great river of life that will flow from the throne to this New Jerusalem (we'll read more about that in the last chapter). God is making everything new as He says in 21:5. But most importantly, all of God's people are finally together and home to live with Christ forever. This is something wonderful to look forward to.

Not only will there be a new earth, but there will also be a New Jerusalem - a totally new, holy city. John mentions that her descent is *"coming down out of heaven from God."* Revelation 21:2

The saints will no longer ascend to the Holy City; it will descend to them on the new earth and be the glorious capital city. New Jerusalem is coming down out of heaven. This may surprise you, because as a believer you may have thought you'll spend eternity up in heaven. This is temporary. God's eternal home will be with you in His eternal city, which will come down out of heaven to God's new earth.[2]

In addition to the new heaven, new earth and New Jerusalem, John observes that there also will be a new order. He hears a loud voice proclaiming the most wonderful thing:

"...now the dwelling of God is with men."

Revelation 21:3

We usually think that the dwelling of men is up in heaven with God for eternity. But here it is in plain words: God will leave heaven and come down to dwell with humans, in the new city, forever. *"He will live with them."*

Another aspect of the new order is the absence of sorrow and pain. God *"will wipe away every tear."* (21:4) *Every* tear. God states, *"His words are trustworthy and true."* Then He addresses the thirsty in 21:6; *"To him who is thirsty, I will give drink without cost from the spring of the water of life. He who overcomes will inherit all this, and I will be his God and he will be my son."* This is the way to eternal life to those who thirst for hunger and righteousness. The people who overcame their sin by choosing Jesus are promised that their thirst will be satisfied forever.

But God also gives a warning to the ones who don't, and He calls them cowards in 21:8. In short, He is saying to those who fill themselves daily on the passions of this life will be sent to a place of eternal torment. These are God's own words speaking to us. No one "accidentally" receives eternal life. It is reserved for those who recognize their need (the thirsty) and demonstrate their faith (who overcomes).

Here's another way to say it; either the sinner will bear his own penalty or Christ will have borne it for him - but the penalty will be paid.

Christian author and preacher Max Lucado tells a story of his friend, Joy, a Sunday school teacher in a poor, inner-city neighborhood. Joy, had a nine year old student whose home life left her afraid and insecure. Her name was Barbara, and she never spoke. While others talked, sang and giggled, Barbara would sit listening and speechless. Then one day, Joy taught a lesson on heaven - a place of tearless eyes and deathless lives. Barbara listened eagerly. Then she raised her hand, asking, "Miss Joy?" Joy was stunned. The girl had never before said a word. "Yes, Barbara?" she replied. Barbara asked, "Is heaven for girls like me?" Heaven is indeed for Barbara and those like her.[3]

What a hopeful thought. God has a wonderful eternity planned for us. We can rejoice and take hope in the fact that our pain is not forever. Just think, no more cancer or disease, no more divorce and heartache, no more poverty and sadness. Just fill in the blank here and think - 'there will be no more of that.' What a happy thought!

God in all His glory, will dwell with us in a close and intimate way that we cannot even imagine. He will bring us to glory with Him, and all the pain will be gone. His heart has been to dwell with us too. What a wonderful time this will be when we will have that close relationship with God just like Adam did before the fall of man. Halleluiah! He is making everything new.

He Who Overcomes

This whole section is to reiterate (if you didn't get it before), that God would love for no one to perish. For he who overcomes, God has this incredible New Jerusalem, with roads to walk on, hills to climb, the best of everything, just waiting for him who believes. If you believe in Jesus Christ as your Savior and know He is the Son of God who came and died for you, then you have overcome your unbelieving heart. Therefore, through faith, you are an overcomer.

An angel tells John that he will show him the bride, the wife of the Lamb. Here, the angel says the city is the bride. Earlier the church is described as the bride. Which is it? Well, it's both.

If I say that Philadelphia is the city of brotherly love, am I describing the physical city or just the people? Both. The city is the bride; the bride is the city.[4]

Then John is taken to a high mountain in 21:10 and there he sees the great city coming down out of heaven. John describes the layout of the city in 21:11-21. To get the full effect of this, I suggest you go back and re-read verses 11-21 again. I'm going to touch on the main descriptions, but it is worth your while to read the detail with which God uses to create this New Jerusalem.

John begins by saying it:

> " shone the glory of God and its brilliance was like that of a very precious jewel…"

Revelation 21:11

I could just stop right there. *"Glory of God"*… *"brilliance"*… *"precious jewel"*… Wow!

Here are just the basics:

- The city was laid out like a square. It was as long as it was wide. The city was 12,000 stadia in length, and as wide and high as it is long. That translates to approximately 1,400 miles long, high, and wide.[5] It is a perfect square (or cube).
- The city had four great walls 144 cubits thick,[6] that's 200 ft thick. That is two-thirds the size of a football field. Just picture that!
- There were three gates on each wall covering the north, south, east and west sides (21:13) equaling 12 in total, and they had the names of the 12 tribes on the gates.
- There were 12 foundations that held the names of the 12 apostles.
- All of these are described as being covered with precious gems and pearls.

The 12 Tribes and 12 Apostles are a picture of the Old and New Covenants united together, united forever. Think about it, there is no Jew, no Gentile - only people of God.

I'm sure you're wondering why are there walls if this is a sinless place? Good question. Commentator Timothy Crater explains it best this way:

> *"The walls are not to protect the city from any evil, for there will be none on the new earth. Rather, the wall defines the city's boundaries relative to the rest of the new earth and stands as an eternal, commemorative site for Israel and the church."*[7]

Now, for fun; some researchers say that the world's population could fit in Texas (think New York high rises covering Texas).[8] Dr. David Jeremiah says that to grasp the enormity of the city of God, think of an area forty times the size of England, or ten times the size of Germany or France. Now take that size and put it over the United States of America. The ground floor alone would provide enough living space for more people than have ever lived in the history of the world. And this is just the first floor! There would still be around 1,300 miles of space for additional floors.[9]

It is an enormous city, surrounded and protected by enormous walls. So, what is my point? Could it be that the enormity of this city reflects the enormity of the love of God that surrounds His children? God is love. A love this great can only be grasped by faith.

John's description is dazzling. He describes walls made of jasper - the city is of pure gold. The foundations are decorated with every imaginable precious stone. It has pearly gates and a street paved with gold. The multi-colored radiance, of such gems brings to mind the wealth and value that God has invested in His eternal city, this investment is for us.

Think of birthstones of today. I love to go in to jewelry stores and see all of the brilliant sparkling gemstones. They look so radiant and glorious. These are the kinds of things that God is laying the foundation of His city with. These gems are precious and valued, like we are to Him.

In Exodus 28:17-20 the Lord gives instructions on how to make the priest's breast piece:

> *"Then they mounted four rows of precious stones on it. In the first row there was a ruby, a topaz and a beryl; in the second row a turquoise, a sapphire and an emerald; in the third row a jacinth, an agate and an amethyst; in the fourth row a chrysolite, an onyx and a jasper. They were mounted in gold filigree settings. There were twelve stones, one for each of the names of the sons of Israel, each engraved like a seal with the name of one of the twelve tribes."*

This is how He dressed his priests - with precious gems. He spares no expense on them. They were valued with valuable stones. He has done the same for our future home.

Years ago, I had the honor of being a teaching director of God's Word for a wonderful organization. As part of our training, we were flown to Colorado. I was overwhelmed by how well they took care of us there. They put us in the best hotel with a five star rating. The food was exquisite as was the service. They spared no expense. I was made to feel I mattered. Heaven is like this too. We will not be floating on clouds and just playing harps. There will be streets of gold to walk through, hills to climb, a whole new earth to explore. We should be excited to spend eternity there. God has spared no expense to lavish His great love on us. Why? Because we matter to God. *You* matter to God.

In the beginning God created the first heaven and earth, and came down to walk with man. After sin was committed, this was no longer possible. God is sinless and cannot dwell where sin is present. So we were stranded down here, but God never wanted this for us. He came down in the flesh and took care of the sin that separates us from Him. Now, when it is time for the new creation - the new heaven and earth - He will come down to dwell with us again, in a city that He has prepared for us and sends down to us. This is how great He loves us!

I find it interesting that the city is made of pure gold and the gates are made of pearls. The way to get gold to be pure is to boil it so all the impurities come to the top. The way a pearl is made is through agitation inside the oyster. I consider these to be tests. Every test and temptation can be a part of God's process of conforming us to the likeness of Christ. Bible teacher Phyllis Cooper says:

> *"So thank Him for the hard times. The enemy will mean them for evil, but God is molding us, sculpting our lives into works of art that will fit in with heaven's beauty."*[2]

The city may be adorned with these precious gems, but they are only a reflection of how precious you are to God. He values His eternal relationship with you. He will spare no cost in order to spend eternity with you.

Think about it - has God not already sent His most precious possession to us - *Jesus Christ* to die for us, that we, through faith, might be saved?

He is always there, hoping and desiring we turn to Him. Loving us ...*always*.

Endnotes:

1. Kendall Easely, Revelation- Holman New Testament Commentary 1998 B & H Publishing Group; Nashville,TN; pg 392-93
2. Community Bible Study TD Helps; 2009; Lesson 27; pg 71
3. Ibid, pg 71
4. Ibid, pg.
5. NIV Study Bible copyright 1985 by The Zondervan Corporation pg. 1949
6. Ibid, pg 1949
7. Community Bible Study Revelation, by Timothy Crater 1997-2004, Lesson 28, pg 3
8. https://www.google.com/search?q=world+population+texas&ie=utf-8&oe=utf-8 & http://www.omgfacts.com/lists/10333/The-entire-world-population-could-fit-in-the-state-of-Texas-and-it-d-only-have-the-population-density-of-New-York-City-ab731-4
9. Community Bible Study TD Helps; 2009; Lesson 28; pg 74

CHAPTER 22

The notion of a garden-like paradise that was lost due to the fall of man still exerts a strong influence on three of the world's major religions: Judaism, Islam and Christianity.

Just think about a few of the themes of Eden:

- Human beings, when given the opportunity, rebel against God, our Creator.
- The serpent continually tries to pull people away from God.
- The curse on the human race includes the banishment from paradise.
- Humans are barred from the Tree of Life.
- Pain and suffering are all around mankind.
- One day "the seed of the woman" will prevail.

By the time the final vision of Revelation ends, these have all been resolved.

- God's people serve Him forever for all rebellion has ceased.
- The serpent has been thrown into the fiery lake forever.
- *"No longer will there be any curse."* (22:3)
- The Tree of Life appears once more, with its fruit.
- God has removed all pain and suffering from His people.
- Jesus, *"the seed of the woman,"* rules from eternity's throne.

Just as the New Jerusalem surpasses Solomon's Jerusalem, as a diamond surpasses a rhinestone, so the new paradise surpasses the old one. This is paradise regained.[1]

The River of Life

Genesis describes Eden as having had a life-giving river that nourished the garden. Now a life-giving river here nourishes the New Jerusalem. Another Old Testament river parallels this too. Ezekiel prophesied a river flowing from the temple of the restored earthly Jerusalem.

> "Fruit trees of all kinds will grow on both banks of the river. Their leaves will not wither, nor will their fruit fail. Every month they will bear fruit, because the water from the sanctuary flows to them, Their fruit will serve for food and their leaves for healing."
>
> Ezekiel 47:12

In Genesis 2:10, the river that is mentioned in the Garden of Eden - "a river watering the garden flowed from Eden," - is a reminder that God has brought human history back to His original intent.

This water is clear as crystal and not polluted, it is neither defiled nor impure. It could not be any other way - its source is from the throne of God. Remember, the new earth has no oceans, only a pure river, which we can use to find our way through the city, and then to the throne of God.

The Tree of Life

Like the water of life, the tree of life symbolizes God's provision of eternal life to His people (just as today the communion sacrament symbolizes Christ's death on our behalf).

The tree of life is again accessible to us only because the Lamb overcame the barrier of sin and death that kept Adam's family from eating its fruit. By taking on Adam's curse as He hung on a tree, the Lamb redeemed His people from the curse and restored their access to the tree of life. His ascent to the tree of death gives us access to the tree of life.[3]

In 22:2 it mentions that the leaves of the tree are for the "...healing of the nations." Ezekiel's prophecy spoke of healing as well.

> "Their fruit will serve for food and their leaves for healing."
>
> Ezekiel 47:12

It seems to me that just as God is providing fruit and water to symbolize life giving sources, He is now providing healing too. Maybe the leaves will be an everlasting memorial to the healing God has provided for all of mankind's mistakes and our infirmities.

"He [Christ] took up our infirmities and carried our diseases."

Matthew 8:17

"...by His wounds we are healed."

Isaiah 53:5

The fruit of the tree grows new crops every month. This suggests an abundance of life as Christ promised.[4]

"...I have come that you may have life and have it to the full."

John 10:10

This tree is planted close to the water source - the river of life. If we apply this lesson to ourselves and stay close to Christ (our source of life), our lives will bear abundant fruit.

Jeremiah makes this same point;

> *"But blessed is the one who trusts in the Lord, whose confidence is in Him. They will be like a tree planted by the water that sends out its roots by the stream. It does not fear when heat comes; its leaves are always green. It has no worries in a year of drought and never fails to bear fruit."*

Jeremiah 17:7-8

This is something we all can aspire to. There is such blessedness here in heaven. There is no more decay, corruption or death - in other words, no curses of any kind. We will see His face. He will live among us. His glory will be our light. He will reign forever.

One commentator said it this way:

> *"The failure in the Garden of Eden is remedied by the success in the Garden of Gethsemane. The death that resulted from taking of the forbidden tree in Eden is conquered by Christ's tree at Calvary."*[5]

Jesus, the Lamb, has accomplished great things on our behalf. The description of life in the New Jerusalem from God to John is now complete. Now the angel authenticates what has just been revealed to John:

> *"The angel said to me, 'These words are trustworthy and true. The Lord, the God who inspires the prophets, sent his angel to show His servants the things that must soon take place. Look, I am*

coming soon. Blessed is the one who keeps the words of the prophecy written in this scroll.'"

Revelation 22:6-7

What is here is authentic, prophetic and truth. How can I say that? It's because of its divine origin. These are the words from our Creator, our God, our Father.

Jesus promises repeatedly that He is coming soon, and that His coming will not be gradual:

"Now, brothers and sisters, about times and dates we do not need to write to you, for you know very well that the day of the Lord will come like a thief in the night. While people are saying, "Peace and safety," destruction will come on them suddenly, as labor pains on a pregnant woman, and they will not escape. But you, brothers and sisters, are not in darkness so that this day should surprise you like a thief."

1 Thessalonians 5:1-4

Are we living with readiness in mind? Jesus reminds us in a parable that it is important to be ready in our waiting.

"At that time the kingdom of heaven will be like ten virgins who took their lamps and went out to meet the bridegroom. Five of them were foolish and five were wise. The foolish ones took their lamps but did not take any oil with them. The wise ones, however, took oil in jars along with their lamps. The bridegroom was a long time in coming, and they all became drowsy and fell asleep.
At midnight the cry rang out: 'Here's the bridegroom. Come out to meet him.'
Then all the virgins woke up and trimmed their lamps. The foolish ones said to the wise, 'Give us some of your oil; our lamps are going out.'
'No,' they replied, 'there may not be enough for both us and you. Instead, go to those who sell oil and buy some for yourselves.'
But while they were on their way to buy the oil, the bridegroom arrived. The virgins who were ready went in with him to the wedding banquet. And the door was shut.
Later the others also came. 'Lord, Lord,' they said, 'open the door for us.'
But he replied, 'Truly I tell you, I don't know you.'

> *Therefore keep watch, because you do not know the day or the hour."*
>
> Matthew 25:1-13

Let this thought challenge us all. Are we living a life ready? In this day and age, this is a good question to be asking ourselves.

As awesome as the Apostle John is, he is still…well…*human*, and he falls down at the feet of the angel to worship him. Many commentators criticize John here in 22:8, but I personally give him grace because he has seen these astounding visions that have filled his heart. He is overwhelmed (wouldn't you be?). However, he is also reminded very sternly that this is inappropriate behavior on his part toward an angel. Angels are just another created being from God. Our focus of worship must be on God alone, the only One worthy of adoration and worship of any kind.

The angel gives instruction to leave the seal of this book open. This is in sharp contrast of what the angel said to Daniel years earlier.

> *"Seal up the vision, for it concerns the distant future…"*
>
> Daniel 8:26

But this angel tells John:

> *"Do not seal up the words of the prophecy of this book, because the time is near."*
>
> Revelation 22:10

God wishes for no one to perish. Keep the seal of this prophecy open so all can hear and (hopefully) repent and change. This is God's heart. This is the reason for the visions of Revelation. It's because He loves us all so much and wants us to be with Him.

The angel is no longer speaking. It is Jesus who speaks now.

> *"Look, I am coming soon. My reward is with Me, and I will give to each person according to what they have done. I am the Alpha and the Omega, the First and the Last, the Beginning and the End."*
>
> Revelation 22:12-13

We are reminded that God is just and judge. First, Christ will judge the repentant. We are all sinners and fall short. But if we are truly repentant of our sins, there are blessings that await us. If not, then judgment and separation from God await us in hell. It's one or the other, but you get to choose.

In 22:15, Jesus talks about those outside - the evildoers who practice magic arts or sexual immorality, the murderers, and so on. Now you might be thinking, can't someone whose committed murder be forgiven? Yes. Of course! You see, there is a difference between someone who has lied, and *a liar*; someone who has murdered, and *a murderer*. It's all a matter of the heart's condition. The evildoer is the one who *"loves and practices falsehoods."* (Rev.22:15) These are the dogs that Jesus is referring too.

Jesus concludes to John that He initiated the writing of this book by sending His angel to give John *"this testimony to the churches."* (Remember the seven churches this is going out to?) Jesus provides the Church with information about the end times in advance so it might prepare itself.

> *"The revelation from Jesus Christ, which God gave him to show his servants what must soon take place. He made it known by sending his angel to his servant John."*
>
> Revelation 1:1

In the beginning of Revelation, there was a blessing for all who would read and or hear this book.

> *"Blessed is the one who reads aloud the words of this prophecy, and blessed are those who hear it and take to heart what is written in it, because the time is near."*
>
> Revelation 1:3

Here, at the end of this book, there is also a warning given to all who read and/or hear these words:

> *"I warn everyone who hears the words of the prophecy of this scroll: If anyone adds anything to them, God will add to that person the plagues described in this scroll. And if anyone takes words away from this scroll of prophecy, God will take away from that person any share in the tree of life and in the Holy City, which are described in this scroll."*
>
> Revelation 22:18-19

This book was given to help the saints, and God will not permit its value to be diminished. The visions are over and the writings are concluding. John had just been given the greatest glimpse of eternal glory that anyone has ever seen. And now, so have we.

He ends with a blessing to us - for all of us who testify that His Word is true and that Jesus is coming soon.

"The grace of the Lord Jesus be with God's people."

And all God's people said, "Amen." AMEN! Revelation 22:21

Truly believing and living in light of this one glorious fact - Jesus is coming soon - can transform our priorities, our view of the world, our hope for the future and our lives. What a hope to hold on to. Maranantha!

In Aramaic "marana" means, our Lord, and "tha" means, come. Maranatha! *Our Lord Come.*

Before we close, I want those who have never read the book of Revelation before, to know that despite all the plagues and judgments - this book is first and formost a divine love story. There are blessings and promises in it, made to you, in the form of Beatitudes.

What is a beatitude? According to dictionary.com it is:

1. supreme blessedness; exalted happiness.
2. any of the declarations of blessedness pronounced by Jesus in the Sermon on the Mount.[6]

In Matthew 5:3-12, as Jesus begins His famous Sermon on the Mount, He lists His eight beatitudes. In Revelation, there are seven. Seven wonderful promises for us! These are ways to experience true joy, and in some cases, avoid real grief.

Here are "The Seven Beatitudes of Revelation"

1. *"Blessed is the one who reads aloud the words of this prophecy, and blessed are those who hear it and take to heart what is written in it, because the time is near."* (1:3) (Blessed is the one who reads, hears and ingests this Word.)
2. *"Blessed are the dead who die in the Lord from now on. They will rest from their labor, for their deeds will follow them."* (14:13) (If you have the Lord in your heart, don't fear death.)
3. *"Look, I come like a thief. Blessed is the one who stays awake and remains clothed, so as not to go naked and be shamefully exposed."* (16:15) (Stay in the Word. Keep the knowledge of God flowing.)
4. *"Blessed are those who are invited to the wedding supper of the Lamb. These are the true words of God."* (19:9) (Blessed are the ones who feast with the King who invites them.)

5. *"Blessed and holy are those who share in the first resurrection. The second death has no power over them, but they will be priests of God and of Christ and will reign with him for a thousand years."* (20:6) (Blessed are the ones who will be resurrected. The second death has no power.)

6. *"Look, I am coming soon. Blessed is the one who keeps the words of the prophecy written in this scroll."* (22:7) (Keep the prophecies of this book.)

7. *"Blessed are those who wash their robes, that they may have the right to the tree of life and may go through the gates into the city."* (22:14) (Blessed are those who enter heaven and live forever.)[7]

At the beginning of this book, we read Psalm 46. I want you to read it once again, now that you have studied and read through the book of Revelation. The Psalm takes on a deeper meaning when read with the knowledge of this book.

God is our refuge and strength,
an ever-present help in trouble.
Therefore we will not fear, though the earth give way
and the mountains fall into the heart of the sea,
though its waters roar and foam
and the mountains quake with their surging.
There is a river whose streams make glad the city of God,
the holy place where the Most High dwells.
God is within her, she will not fall;
God will help her at break of day.
Nations are in uproar, kingdoms fall;
he lifts his voice, the earth melts.
The Lord Almighty is with us;
the God of Jacob is our fortress.
Come and see what the Lord has done,
the desolations he has brought on the earth.
He makes wars cease
to the ends of the earth.
He breaks the bow and shatters the spear;
he burns the shields with fire.
He says, "Be still, and know that I am God;
I will be exalted among the nations,
I will be exalted in the earth."
The Lord Almighty is with us;
the God of Jacob is our fortress.

Psalm 46

Endnotes:

1. Kendall Easely, Revelation- Holman New Testament Commentary 1998 B & H Publishing Group; Nashville,TN; pg 413
2. Community Bible Study, Revelation, commentary by Phyllis Cooper, 1997-2004, Lesson 29 pg 4
3. Community Bible Study, Revelation by commentary by Timothy Crater, 1997-2004, Lesson 29, pg 5
4. Ibid., pg 5
5. Ibid., pg 7
6. Dictionary.com
7. Engaging God's Word: Revelation, copyright 2012 by Community Bible Study

CONCLUSION

My hope as you have read this companion study, is that you come to a clearer understanding of just how much God loves you. His heart is for no one to perish. But He is not a puppeteer and we are not His puppets. There is free will involved. My hope is for you to see that He is a just God, and that there is a plan for this world and sadly, it is to end. But that is so a new one can begin again. We seem to forget that part.

This book is not just about all of the judgments and plagues to come. That is only part of the big puzzle. This is not our home, heaven is. We must think *heavenly minded*.

My prayer for you today, is for you to feel closer to God and begin to understand His heart for you, and as a result be motivated to go deeper with Him. Find a Bible study. Get involved in the Word. Let His book of Revelation be a revelation to you of His mighty love. He loves you so much! Remember that and let His love take root in your heart.

God bless you!

About the Author

Jill Grossman is an author, speaker and teacher from Nashville, Tennessee. She and her husband Steve are co-directors of Family Life Ministries at their church which provides premarital, marriage and family support. Their weekly blogs can be found online at: www.family.stevegrossmanonline.com.

Steve and Jill have been married for 30 yrs and have two adult children, Kayce and Jennah.

Jill is currently pursuing a B.A. in Pastoral Christian Counseling. She also enjoys acting, singing, dancing and gardening.

WordCrafts Press

Pro-Verb Ponderings
31 Ruminations on Positive Action
by Rodney Boyd

Morning Mist
Stories from the Water's Edge
by Barbie Loflin

Why I Failed in the Music Business
and how NOT to follow in my footsteps
by Steve Grossman

Youth Ministry is Easy!
and 9 other lies
by Aaron Shaver

Chronicles of a Believer
by Don McCain

Illuminations
by Paula K. Parker & Tracy Sugg

A Scarlet Cord of Hope
By Sheryl Griffin

www.wordcrafts.net

80288740R00119

Made in the USA
Lexington, KY
01 February 2018